CW00468122

A Mindful Intelligence Title. All rights reserved. 2nd Edition: ISBN 978-0-9940389-2-0, 2024 / 1st Edition limited to 50 copies, 2023

Cover art and cartoon illustrations by Tracy Rowan / Bulk orders through: Ingram or mindfulintelligence.net

MINDFUL INTELLIGENCE
and the making of YOU

WHAT IS MINDFUL INTELLIGENCE, AND WHY DOES IT MATTER?

Mindful Intelligence is a focus on mindfulness, as it relates to creating and understanding the "self." Mindfulness can help a self-concept develop and evolve, but you have to notice and take charge of this process! With mindfulness, you can become aware of your default perceptions and habits so you can adjust them and "who you are," as needed. When you're able to maintain awareness of thoughts, feelings, and actions -as they happen- you can more consciously choose them. Mindful Intelligence helps you understand yourself, and how to evolve as a human being, by giving you the superpower of knowing what you're up to (and why) at all times. Believe it or not, this doesn't happen by default!

WHAT IS MINDFULNESS?

Mindfulness is paying attention to your experience on purpose, in the present moment. Mindful practice hones the awareness, and helps you understand how to best use your mind, given that thoughts lead to feelings, actions, and ultimately who you are in this life. Mindfulness is used by Yogis to refine their thoughts and behaviour on the path to enlightenment, and it can be used by you for the same purpose. If you're aiming low you can use mindfulness to relieve stress, gain integrity and confidence, and feel more joy in everyday life. If you're aiming high, not even the sky is the limit.

Contents

INTRODUCTION

People's ability to deceive themselves *about themselves* caught my attention and wouldn't let go when I was a teenager.

It was the early 90's, I worked at a Retirement Home in the summers, and my favorite thing to do there was people-watching. I expected the elderly residents to be wise, and some were, but I was surprised by the number of people at death's door who still behaved in childish ways. I'm not referring to those living with the effects of pain or dementia, but healthy people who lacked the maturity of their years. It was my introduction to the reality that people can live an entire lifetime without figuring themselves out.

There were residents who bickered, blamed, gossiped, and battled over love interests. I was looking for intellectual stimulation and perhaps a bit of guidance, but more often than not I got a soap opera with an interesting cast. With a non-stop rotation of visitors, Residents, Nurses, Doctors, Support

Workers, Janitors, Cooks, Therapists, Ministers, Undertakers, and visiting animals, there was the potential for major drama on any given shift.

One of my favorite "characters" was a cantankerous Resident named Delores. When Delores talked about her useless daughters, the incompetent staff, and my own failings (ad nauseam) it was obvious something about her thinking was off.

MORE TEA!!
YOU INCOMPETENT
LAZY
NO ACCOUNT
GOOD FOR NOTHING
PRISSY NURSE!

She wasn't senile. Delores was so with it, she could smell fear on you. She knew what everyone was doing without setting foot outside her room. Delores wasn't the only person in my orbit with a questionable character, but seeing that character alone on her death bed made a big impression.

It eventually became clear that Delores carried around a lifetime of emotional baggage and either didn't know it, or thought it had nothing to do with her. Delores spent a great deal of time convincing herself and anyone who'd listen that other people were responsible for her problems.

This caught my attention because I'd been brought up to believe I was responsible for my own misery and happiness. Six siblings and I were all told the same thing about whining: If you're not content it's your problem. Either sort yourself out or get something to whine about, like two hours of cutting the grass, or weeding the garden in blackfly season.

A similar no-nonsense policy applied to fighting: "Stop it or you're all in trouble!" The lack of sensitivity was balanced by practical wisdom. An 'at-your-own-risk' stance on whining and fighting sent a clear message: It's not a useful way to get your needs met, so stop doing it. There was zero room for blame, self-pity, or lack of personal responsibility.

Given my encounters with Delores, I started to wonder how often people spend their entire lives dissatisfied, believing change is impossible because they don't realize they (and not others) are required to make the changes.

To investigate, I used the next decade of my life and relationships to work out some of the psychological mysteries. I covertly observed people's lives and choices with the finely tuned people-watching skills of a serious introvert. Eventually I had counselling clients so I could people-watch for a living.

I noticed many people in Western Society look outside the "self" for answers when problems arise. Something goes wrong or feels uncomfortable, and an external search for clues kicks into high gear. Who has done me wrong? Do I need a better job, spouse, tv, or exercise regimen? Good weather, sympathy, chocolate, recognition, mega-house, pills, money, lover, wine, understanding, something super-sized? What?

It's easy to look outside the self to lay blame or find answers, because the world is so compelling, and the inner world of mind/emotions is subtle. Most of Western culture focuses primarily on material development rather than emotional or spiritual development, so the inner self isn't always seen as the prime mover it is.

A mindful approach is to look for answers in your thoughts and feelings first, because everything you do starts from within. The inner self is you in thoughts/feelings/values, and the outer self is you in the material world of action. The overall sense of self is built gradually from interplay between the inner and outer self, *but you have to pay attention to notice it.* This is where Mindful Intelligence comes in.

Unfortunately, the awareness of self is not always complete or coherent enough to help people live each day with conscious intention, and the possibility of developing the self is not on everyone's radar. Stress or anxiety, lack of input (experience/support), and acquired habits can easily prevent development, understanding, and even awareness of the self. As you might imagine, lack of self-awareness is at the crux of human struggles.

Sometimes people don't notice how much they struggle because they're too busy struggling to notice things. *This book encourages noticing things.* The degree to which you develop your inner self (in thoughts/feelings/values) and notice how the inner and outer self work together, makes you mindful or not so mindful of what you think, feel, and do.

It can be tempting to think others or outside circumstances run your life or cause your problems, but it's not an accurate picture of reality. The self is the one thing you have control over (potentially) and the self is a key player in any issue it's involved with, so it makes sense to focus your attention there.

We often think our better half, the boss, kids, parents, time, or some other malevolent force is the problem, or in charge of how we feel, but this is a perspective problem worth fixing. If someone is driving you down a road you don't like, it's up to you to get out of the car, and run back to town. There's always something you can think (or not think), feel (or not feel), do (or not do), to adjust your experience.

Making yourself responsible to focus on what *you* can do to improve things -in each moment- makes more sense than thinking someone else or the world should change first. Yet, how often is our default feeling that we *have to* do things, as if we're victims of some external "other" that controls us?

How often in frustration do we only focus on what the other person, or the world, should be doing to improve things? We could all keep waiting for that, but we'll be waiting for a very long time.

Delores was convinced the world and everyone in it was against her, because she took no responsibility for how her thoughts, feelings, actions, and values, created her reality. She was driving her life but didn't know she was at the wheel.

Through Mindful Intelligence, anyone can take more positive control of both the inner and outer self, and refine subtle aspects of that self over time. Delores' lack of responsibility and self-awareness was extreme, but it's common human behaviour to abdicate responsibility for some things, and creatively avoid other things, while keeping these facts hidden from yourself. The human mind is truly a complex wonder!

In short, when you catch yourself behaving like Delores, using blame or fighting instead of constructive problem-solving, that's your cue to look within. This is where you observe how your thoughts lead to feelings and actions, so you can refine your thinking and leave unconscious reactions behind.

As a guage to know if your inner self needs work, would it be okay if everyone could hear your thoughts? Anything unethical in there? Any conflict, confusion, obsession, fear, inconsistency or resentment? Daydreaming instead of doing? Spinning thoughts vs. calm focus? Save the princess fantasy?

A mindfully intelligent life is about honestly facing your struggles and contradictions without fear, so you can improve your quality of life. If one day you notice you are filled with bliss while simply feeling your body move and breathe, it will mark your arrival at the heart of mindful practice.

Part One of this book illuminates the wonders of Mindfulness and how they relate to "the making of you." Part Two shows how to work with over fifty attitudes and actions/reactions, each with a two page spread, with illustrative cartoon on the left, and description with practices on the right. The 52 topics help you think about how to evolve both inwardly (inner self) and outwardly (in relationships/actions). I illustrated the cartoons to show the most important thing I learned about each topic, through mindful practice.

You may also choose an attitude or reaction to work on, and use more suggested practices in the back of the book. These are compilations of ideas and practices I've picked up over the years, which have effectively hooked me on mindfulness for twenty-five years (so far). This book is a companion to the 'Mindful on the Move' app that goes further into the topics, and how they can be worked with during everyday life. See the last page for details.

Mindfulness helps you build a strong sense of self by encouraging you to develop thoughts, feelings, and actions from the inside-out (proactive), instead of the outside-in (reactive). It reminds you to keep an eye on the medium your life is being filtered through: you. Ultimately, mindful intelligence helps you fully appreciate life while noticing how the self interacts with, and creates that life.

Thanks to Delores for inspiring this book!

DELORES AND HER "BAGGAGE," SHE CARRIED IT ALWAYS.

When transforming thoughts and feelings into actions, you can tell yourself one or more lies, or gloss over pertinent details.

THE COMPLEX MIND AND THE INTENTIONAL SELF

Most people aren't aware of how they use their minds in enough detail to honestly say they're running all aspects of their lives with conscious intention.

Observing the self is a purposeful act. The default human setting is more likely to pay attention to external events or others than to do accurate self-analysis. Generally, people think they're in control of themselves, and they seem to be doing things "on purpose," but the separate elements of the self: mind, emotions, body, and soul aren't always on the same page.

The mind can misinterpret or totally ignore emotions and other "uncomfortable" information, so doing things on purpose or with righteous intent, isn't as straight-forward as it sounds. This is why it's possible to behave one way and feel bad about it later. Sometimes when transforming thoughts and feelings into actions, you can tell yourself one or more lies, or gloss over pertinent details.

When you aren't fully aware of how your thoughts and feelings lead to intentions and actions -in each moment- you aren't in complete control of yourself. People are used to hearing they should be aware of the motives behind their actions, but how often are they? When a fighting couple slings insults at each other, are they aware of their motives for doing that, or how this behaviour connects to what they want from life overall?

Does it make sense to attack the person you're supposed to love, honour, and protect, or to harm the person you want to love and protect you? If not, why do people do it?

In mid-fight, if people were fully aware of their thoughts, feelings and intentions, they'd look something like this: I'm going to make you understand I'm the victim here, even if I have to yell and scream and hurt you back. I am justified because you won't listen or apologize.

The problem is both parties think the same thing, so you have two "justified" people arguing about how one hurt trumps the other. But isn't there room for both people to speak about needs and hurts, and room for two apologies?

Competitive thinking says no. There is one winner, one loser. You only have room for two hurts and two apologies with the more advanced relationship strategy that values cooperation over competition. Cooperation makes more sense in a partnership, because if both sides don't win to some extent, the health and stability of the partnership is diminished.

Cooperative thinking allows more than one way of doing things, and more than one perspective. Instead of turning someone who disagrees into an enemy, cooperative thinking uses mutual respect and humility to protect the rights and feelings of both sides.

For cooperative thinking to take hold, you need to self-reflect and become aware of your more selfish (self-protective), reactive thinking. This is a basic requirement of Mindful Intelligence;

the willingness to look at, and take responsibility for, your less admirable qualities.

Reactive thoughts, feelings, and actions, come from insecurities or vulnerabilities created in the past. Defensive insecurities make you feel like you have to do things like shut down dissenting opinions, or prove your victim feelings are justified at all costs. People who think bullying is a legitimate social (or political) strategy were victimized in the past, and they believe taking things by force is the only way to get their needs met.

The problem with this reasoning and behaviour is it's hypocritical, because bullies don't like being bullied either. The ability to separate pain from the past (and the resulting defenses), from what is happening right now, is an ongoing exercise in mindfulness. It determines who you will be in each moment, and how lost in pain, or loving and joyful you can be.

In the heat of the average fight most people don't acknowledge wrongdoing on their part because they're focused on the wrong that was done to them. They're focused on defending and reacting.

The mindful approach is to stay aware of your thoughts, feelings, and motives, so you can communicate with the same respect you'd like for yourself- regardless of what the other person is doing. Most fighting hinges on the idea that bad behaviour is justified by other bad behaviour. With mindful attention, it becomes clear that the only true way to win a fight, or indeed to win at life overall, is to behave with integrity, regardless of other people's choices.

Our opinions and perceptions are often skewed by personal bias because in our minds we're at the center of our own private universe.

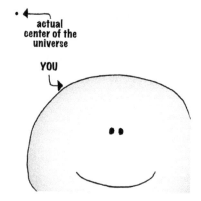

Self reflection and empathy for others is needed to balance this bias toward the self and create humility. The fact that we rule our brains in the ongoing private conversation with ourselves, tends to make us think we're untouchable royalty. On the throne in our private minds, we can tell people off, succeed at things we'll never do, and congratulate ourselves repeatedly.

Humility is realizing this throne in your mind doesn't exist, neither does the Kingdom, nor the staff who make it all possible. It's realizing how equal you are with everyone on the planet, and then treating yourself and others accordingly.

When feeling over-confident, people behave as if they're at the center of the universe looking out at the deluded masses, and when feeling under-confident, people are upset at how the masses look at them funny. Both over-confidence and under-confidence are delusions caused by having an inaccurate, self-focused, general *idea* of "me."

A general concept of "me" is the set-up for perceiving others as stereotyped "them," the opposing force in the aforementioned competitive thinking. The more honest, detailed understanding people have of themselves and their concept "me," the more they can understand and respect the complexity of others.

Mindful Intelligence gets you past the general concept of me, and into your thoughts where you're creating "you" moment by moment. The most true you exists at the soul level, and the ego you is alive in your thoughts and habits. When you can see how your ego operates moment to moment, you learn to relax it, so your soul can shine through more often.

You can cross the line from thinking of yourself as a static entity known as "me" to the knowledge that you are a product of your choices -moment by moment- fully responsible for your ongoing evolution. This more dynamic sense of "you" feels less like a permanent identity, and more like an energy you can use in your soul's unfolding.

When you observe your thoughts in detail, you realize how important it is to be intentional with them. Default (unintentional) thinking is often comprised of habits, some of which are negative because they formed as a reaction to stress.

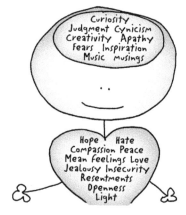

From perfectionism to apathy and everything in between, negative or reactive thinking takes many forms. Negativity not only comments on the issue at hand (I dislike this or that), but points to something problematic about how you focus your attention. Negative, or unconstructive thoughts stand directly in the way of positive, constructive thoughts, which you need to have if you want positive things to happen.

An ongoing "I can't stand that guy" story in your mind, means something about you, and is not just about the guy you don't like. Putting things off isn't about what you put off, and boredom isn't because life is boring (again, all you).

Seeing the direct connection between quality of thoughts, feelings, and quality of life, takes a higher degree of self-awareness and personal responsibility than most people practice. Without detailed self-awareness, it's possible, and even easy, to run through a lifetime without having a solid grasp on what you're doing.

Getting to know some of the uglier details of the self is a small price to pay for true personal integrity and living the life you choose on purpose, moment-by-moment. It's often considered necessary to take a non-judgmental inventory of flaws, as a necessary step for growth or healing.[1] Until you identify your default thoughts, attitudes, actions, and reactions, you can't know how they affect you. If you don't know where you are, where is there to go?

WHY AREN'T PEOPLE MINDFULLY INTELLIGENT BY DEFAULT?

Accurate self-understanding only happens after a conscious choice is made to observe the self honestly, over time. In much of Western society, becoming introspective or a person of depth, is not an obvious goal for maturing people.[2]

Many people choose to develop belief systems and personal goals, but with the diminishing tendency to see formal religions, or anything as a moral authority, personal ethics are not always considered or discussed. Even if people subscribe to an ethical belief system, it's not a given that they will apply its principles to their own behaviour in any detail (see religious people who think it's okay to be mean to *those other* people who are not like us).

True personal accountability requires more than ritual behaviours or belonging to a like-minded group. Ethics need to be applied at the mental, emotional, and physical levels of life, and to do that, one needs to be aware (through self-observation) of behaviour patterns in thoughts, feelings and actions.

If people are raised in a tense environment, the focus needed for introspection is often absorbed by defensive habits, anxiety, and other stressors. Another challenge is today's distracting virtual world of computers, consumer ads, and image-over-substance sensational media. In some people, this creates confusion or indifference about whether image is more important than authenticity.

Regarding the "self," this might be seen in a person who puts time into developing a digital persona on social media, while spending little or no time considering the possibility of *actual* character refinement.

A practice like mindfulness that encourages self-reflection and value driven behaviour, can help people develop an internalized sense of meaning that grows with experience, and supports a life built on informed choices.

LACK OF MINDFUL INTELLIGENCE AT A WORLD LEVEL

It's easy to understand why world politics are as messy as they are, if you yourself are sometimes aggressive, dishonest, throwing tantrums, or holding a grudge. When was the last time you issued an ultimatum? And how did that go?

When individuals step-up personal responsibility for mindful behaviour en-masse, politics will shift accordingly. For example, in US politics, many people supported a flimsy apparition of "strong leadership" in Donald Trump (45th President of the United States of America, and frontrunner in the 2024 election). His methods included childish bullying tactics, criminal behaviour, and direct statements of contempt for human rights and the law, flaunted almost daily on social media and news outlets.

It wasn't a lack of accurate information about Trump's behaviour that kept people loyal to him, but rather a lack of interest in accurate information. The Berkeley News article: "Despite drift toward authoritarianism, Trump voters stay loyal, why?" noted the following:

> Gabriel Lenz, an expert in political psychology, is the author of Follow the Leader? How Voters Respond to Politicians' Performance and Policies (University of Chicago Press, 2012)...says political opinion is shaped by an apathetic lack of awareness... many people follow a political party as they would a football team, researchers say. Values may be less important in shaping allegiance than family tradition or the shared identity and social pressures of a community. Lenz and other political scientists call it "rational ignorance."[3]

The phenomenon above is mentioned because, while most who voted for Trump wouldn't say they'd prefer an Authoritarian government, they did in fact vote for one. Trump repeatedly aligned himself with dictators like Vladimir Putin and Kim Jong-un, and then attempted to overturn election results in 2020. When people lose sight of how to reconcile thoughts, feelings and actions coherently with ethics, they can support and end up with things they don't actually want.

WARNING: THE BLAME TRAP (OBSERVING OTHERS INSTEAD OF YOURSELF)

Focusing on what others do (and specifically do wrong) is a very popular pastime. It rivals tv, drugs, money, food, and sex for most popular distractions of all time. Noticing what others do wrong is inevitably followed by noticing how others do *me* wrong.

If you are forever looking out of *what other people do* goggles, or *what people have done to me* coloured glasses, you may be effectively blind to what I do, and what I could be doing better.

People who practice mindful intelligence realize they have enough personal flaws to work on to consume an entire lifetime (or more), so they see the wisdom of ceasing to worry about what everyone else is doing.

Yes it's important to be aware of others and to help right wrongs, but not at the expense of ignoring the wrongs you yourself are involved in. Sometimes people over-focus on others to apparently be helpful, but ignoring yourself and your own issues to focus elsewhere is an avoidance strategy, however helpful it is to others.

If you've accumulated some 'baggage' on the airplane ride of your life, and it sometimes falls down on your head and on the people sitting next to you, don't be afraid to investigate what's going on. Mindful practice can help you learn to travel light again.

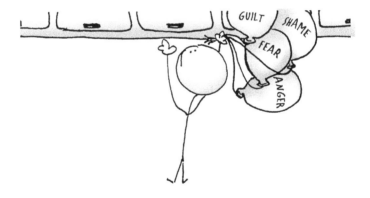

MINDFUL INTELLIGENCE AND STRUGGLE

Mindful intelligence can be applied to every moment, and every conflict that arises. We are conflicted in many moments throughout the day, and conflict presents itself as a feeling of struggle against something. Anything other than pure contentment can be a struggle. Mistrust, irritation, insecurity, avoidance and procrastination are just some of the cues to notice struggle, and then reflect on why you've been thrown off balance.

From waiting to cutting in line, people avoidance, alarms, boredom, spinning thoughts, kids, addiction, loneliness, rushing and road rage, there are potentially hundreds of moments in a day that can be transformed from struggle to contentment by mindful practice.

You might start by noticing the struggles that take up a lot of room in your mind, and use reflection, problem-solving, and practices to help you enjoy more about the present moment. Stress and struggle can obscure everything good in life, and people can be more or less aware of this.

As each struggle is transformed, so are you. With practice, you shift from feeling like someone to whom things happen, to someone who chooses what happens, and how. The goal is not to control everything, but to responsibly and honestly manage "you" as you move through life.

Your attitudes, actions, and reactions can be more or less conscious; more or less based on fear; more or less based on ethics you stand by.

CHANGING THE BRAIN THROUGH MINDFUL PRACTICE

The human brain likes to categorize things, so it easily creates habits. The brain forms strong neural connections between often expressed emotions that are linked to particular thoughts and actions. These connected thoughts/feelings/actions can become automatic *reactions* if you aren't choosing thoughts and behaviours "on purpose."[4]

The same way you have to train the motions and habits of driving to make them easy and effortless, you also train mental-emotional habits, and you need to untrain the unwanted ones. Throughout life, especially in childhood, we are exposed to people and situations we have no control over, which can cause us to form defenses and judgments that still plague us in adult life.

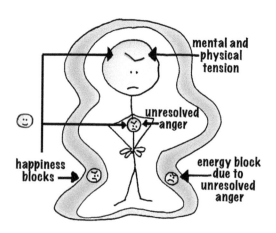

Mindful intelligence builds flexibility into your thinking, so you are no longer held prisoner by mental-emotional reactions from the past. It helps you open your eyes and mind to the fact that each moment is unique, and therefore holds potential.

There are more graceful ways of responding to problems than being aggressive, defensive, apathetic, or hopeless, but if you follow the automatic track of your habits when stressed, you won't see or learn about the other possibilities. You might be constantly fighting stress and automatic mind chatter because a busy mind is all you've ever known. Where does that song you hate come from anyway, and why is it always playing in your mind if you didn't put it there?

With mindful attention on your thoughts, and adjusting your focus through practices, your mind gradually becomes populated with more of what you want, and less of what you don't want. In time it becomes easier to sustain an intentional focus because your brain changes to support your new patterns of focus through neural adjustments (see neuroplasticity).[5]

As noted in Daniel Goleman and Richard Davidson's book Altered Traits, "even beginning meditators have shown less mind-wandering, better focus, and working memory after only two weeks of practice, and small improvements in molecular markers of cellular aging seem to emerge with just thirty hours of practice."[6] De-stressing is an enormous benefit of mindful or meditative practice, which may contribute to positive effects in cellular aging markers.

A mindful focus is a pleasant interplay between what you choose, and what is just there in the moment, waiting for you to notice. This dual awareness replaces the default "busy mind." A loose focus lets you "just be" in the moment, noticing what the world has to offer in a particular moment, and how that marries with your intentions. This is different from the default mind which filters information through a stream of unintentional thoughts and pre-formed judgments from the past.

Non-judgment is a key mindful practice (p.169) that shows you how often your mind projects unnecessary judgments on everything and everyone around you. When practices and eventual brain changes help you release all this thought traffic, you're more immersed in your moments, instead of endless mental projections. Life becomes more full and interesting because you're actually present to experience it.

OVER-FOCUS ON THE NEGATIVE

When you focus too much on negative thoughts, it's self-limiting, in the same way bad weather can make it hard to see or move. How entrenched you are in negativity determines if you're trying to create a positive existence through a fog, hailstorm, or tornado of negative thoughts and emotions.

With mindful intelligence, you work on clearing up the sky of your mind so "being you" is less about getting through a problem and more about enjoying and making the most of "what is." In extreme form, ongoing negativity is a sign of emotional instability or mental illness, but all people have negative thoughts and feelings, and need to consciously work on figuring out their underlying conflicts (popularly known as unfinished business, or baggage), in order to stop overreacting to emotional triggers.

Being either emotionally repressed, or highly emotional can be caused by growing up in a tense household. If you were over-exposed to stress, and under-exposed to various forms of nurturing like emotional support, education, play, kindness, nutrition and safety, you can work on nurturing yourself. Children (and adults) benefit from having boundaries that allow both safety and freedom, to encourage problem-solving and creativity. Emotional regulation involves complex body-mind skills that can be focused on and improved with mindful practice.

IN MINDFUL PRACTICE WE ASK OURSELVES HARD QUESTIONS IN THE MOMENT SUCH AS...

- When uncomfortable, is my first act to blame someone, or to be defensive/reactive in other ways?

- When in a bad mood, hungry, or tired, do I repeat negative stories, resentments, or scenarios in my mind (and dwell on them instead of recognizing the stress behind them)?

- During conflict, do I fail to account for my own participation in problems, or lack of it, while focusing with glaring clarity on other people's flaws (and how dare they)?

- When making choices, do I justify less than pure motives or gloss over inattention to higher ethics or principles?

- When busy, do I get lost in minutia, spinning thoughts, or stress and forget to relax, pay attention to life in a balanced way, or think about what I'm doing with my life overall?

- Balancing relationships with myself and others, do I get caught up in other people's issues and avoid my own? Do I tend to remain stuck or apathetic for long periods? Do the boundaries between my needs and other's seem hard to manage?

- Regarding respect, do I treat people with less respect than I'd like to receive myself, using words that are harsh or dismissive when frustrated, or do I allow this behaviour from others?

- Do I spend time wallowing in self-pity and victim stories about not being treated well enough, to avoid personal responsibility, or do I hang around with people who do?

Yes, sometimes we do these things. Mindfulness is an ongoing practice that protects us choice by choice -moment to moment- from habits that can turn us into people we don't actually want to be.

MINDFUL PERSPECTIVE

Much confusion arises from the skewed perspective of seeing your own analysis of events as being separate from you- the analyzer. As the analyzer of your own experience, you are in fact, very involved in what you're thinking and seeing, moment to moment.

The essence of mindfulness is to always remember it's not about what happens *to you*, it's about how you act and react. In each moment you have two world views to choose from: In one you act, and in the other you react. When you act, the implication is that you act with intention and integrity, not out of habit or because you've been emotionally triggered.

EXAMPLE 1

While being mindful of your train of thought you might notice you spend much of the day thinking about who or what is in your way. You may not have been aware of this, because all your focus was on what was in your way instead of on why you think things are in your way.

Mindfulness can help you shift your attention to the fact that you're in charge of creating (and clearing if necessary) your own path in the world. You can creatively adjust, or step around obstacles rather than dwell on why they exist.

This may seem like a subtle nuance, but it's the difference between people who move toward what they want, and people who remain stuck feeling helpless,...maybe without knowing they feel helpless, because they're focused on being annoyed, disappointed, or reactive in other ways.

EXAMPLE 2

With practice, you may realize that arguing often with someone who won't change or admit fault is not only their defect, but yours as well. Your focus may change from getting this person to agree with you, to asking yourself why am I doing this? Or wouldn't I rather be around someone who has enough humility to admit fault without arguing? Or why can't I state and live my truth calmly without getting caught up in arguing myself?

EXAMPLE 3

Most people care about being basically ethical and kind, but it's many a kind person that has, over the centuries, participated in atrocities. The human mind's capacity to compartmentalize, rationalize, and forget is such that down can seem to be up sometimes. Unless you're being very mindful about what you're thinking and doing, and asking yourself the hard questions, it's difficult to hold yourself to a high standard when the pressure is on.

Would anyone be able to start an unjust war (based on greed and quest for power) if nobody agreed to fight? It's not an easy choice to defy your government, but it's not an easy choice to murder people for questionable reasons either.

Sometimes the protection of family and friends becomes a reason for doing unethical things, or people say they were just following orders at work. Life is full of hard choices, and the more deeply you get into mindful practice, the more you see the importance of thinking critically and proactively about who you are, what you want, and what you say and do.

Mindfulness isn't only about ethics, it's about feeling joy and peace. There is a relaxed and joyous inner peace that comes from refining your "self" and your energy through mindful practice.

The Neuroscientist/author Jill Bolte Taylor, might describe this peace as spending more time in your right brain.[7] Thich Nhat Hanh[8] described how to achieve that peace through practice in everyday moments in his books on mindfulness like "Being Peace," and "Peace is Every Step."

Mindful practice helps you understand that each moment of your life is an opportunity to experience beauty and peace, and if that's not the case, to ask yourself questions like: what is my responsibility in this; is there anything I could change; how can I adjust how I feel; or how can I treat this person better?

Transforming your self over time with mindfulness is about noticing your conflicts and contradictions, and transforming them into habits of mind, body, and soul that agree on how to operate as an integrated, ethical, more easily contented "you."

GOING DEEPER AND DEEPER INTO MEANING WITH MINDFULNESS

A fight breaks out in the kitchen of your home. Who took the last piece of chocolate cake? Without a mindful approach you might merely think about how to protect yourself from being blamed [= the reactive approach]. If you go deeper, you might notice similar petty arguments going on, rather than discussions about meaning and happiness.

You might internally inquire- what does this say about me? What could I do or not do, to adjust how people in my home focus their attention? [= the proactive approach].

While reflecting about how you'd rather be in a household where generosity, forgiveness, and support prevails over petty arguments, you might ask yourself, why isn't this the case already? What are the default beliefs and assumptions that have set up this family habit?

You have all the ingredients in petty squabbles for war: blame, lack of personal responsibility, competitive thinking, a victim and oppressor, and disconnection instead of empathy, kindness, forgiveness, cooperation and solidarity.

How did this war mentality leak into your home? There is something you are doing or not doing that contributes to this reality, but what? Mindful intelligence is an effective tool to investigate such mysteries as these.

You might decide to focus your attention on how you handle conflicts or disagreements, so you can adjust your approach. With your example, the whole household can evolve past competitive thinking to being more cooperative.[9] Doing this is not only a help to the atmosphere in your home, it's the depth of responsibility for one's actions that is required (one person, one household, one group at a time), for the entire world to become more ethical, cooperative, and loving.

In our house, my mom's favorite move was to say something nice about a person if others were being critical. I remember being annoyed by this, on the surface seeing it as a feeble bid for "niceness," but part of me knew there was no good justification for negativity or mean gossip. This is something I reflected on further during my interactions with the inestimable Delores.

My mother's non-violent intervention against judgmental criticism wore me down, the more I thought about it. She led by example and didn't have to directly say anything against what we did. She simply did the more appropriate, ethical thing alongside our thoughtless behaviour.

Leading by example is genius in its simplicity. Instead of directly challenging someone, show them another way. Instead of watching the news and lamenting over sensationalized events, and thinking the world is going "downhill" (a victim's powerless stance), you can clean up the world's problems in your mini world at home.

The people in your home, or circle of influence will go into the world and make families of their own. They'll impact friends and co-workers, and perhaps become leaders in different ways. Seen this way, every gesture and interaction can move the needle on the world goodness scale.

Mindfulness is an empowering practice that counters the illusion that some external "other" is in charge of our lives and causing our problems. Even if we are oppressed by some turn of circumstance or fate, in most situations we still have some dominion over our thoughts, feelings, actions and values.

To the extent that we do, we are free to turn ourselves -moment by moment- into people who live our meaning every day, instead of accidentally wasting life on judgments, fears, negativity and unconscious habits. Do people really accidentally waste life? Yes, they often do.

It's human nature to illogically believe you'll life forever, so people like to ignore mortality until death is upon them. It's better to make friends with death now, because paying attention to life's impermanence helps you see (and make) different choices.

DEATH BED PRACTICE

An important mindful practice is to fast-forward in your mind to the end of your life and acknowledge that your own death will in fact occur. The practice is important because it helps you make more responsible decisions now.

For most people, it's harder to make unethical or harmful decisions if you truly understand your mind/body is here for a limited time only. There is an end to the time you have to do, or undo anything. With this perspective, before doing something atrocious, or merely inconsiderate or ill-advised, you can ask yourself: on my deathbed, will I regret mistreating this person, or turning away from what I know is right?

Another common deathbed thought you'd probably rather not have is: Why didn't I just go for it, why was I afraid to live? Mindful intelligence helps you notice where your weak spots are hidden among your relative strengths, so you can understand them, rather than letting them quietly rule your life in the background.

At minimum you can notice oversights or mistakes soon after you've made them, and try to make them right before the death-bed stage of things. But it's never too late to become a more kind, nuanced, wise person of depth, so you can finish this life knowing you've seen the world, and yourself, through mindfully intelligent eyes.

THE ULTIMATE GOAL OF MINDFULNESS AND MEDITATION

Have you seen someone enter a room and intrigue people with their gravitas, not because they were good looking, telling a great story or in the midst of a scandal, but because the energy they emitted was soft and strong at the same time? This is someone wise enough to be neither self-conscious nor deluded by self-importance. They just "are" and are not trying to "be" anything.

The unique quality of someone with a dialed-down ego is noticeable at a distance. This quality, even more magnified, can be seen and felt in the presence of lifelong meditating Yogis. Their primary focus is to evolve beyond ego conflicts to refine their energy, so they can have access to more spiritual (less material) realms.

In the fiction world, there is Yoda, empowered by 'the force,' Grand Master Jedi on Star Wars. He's ugly, yet adorable. Irresistible because there's a wormhole of wisdom where his fear and ego used to be. Those who possess this mysterious well of wisdom can, without effort, take one look at you and see what fears spin you around.

This kind of clarity comes from having evolved beyond the fears which lay beneath every overreaction. Seeing and accepting things as they are, without fear and struggle has a calming effect. In our energetic world, it can be likened to refining your radio signal so you don't produce so much static. If you take mindful intelligence as far as it can go, you will begin to access information and energy that people with heavy or confused energy can't access.[10]

Knowing you want wisdom more than anything else the world offers means you've glimpsed a truth that many others miss while focusing on material world shiny things. The state of your mind and soul matters, and if you wait until your fatal disease diagnosis to whip yourself into shape for the death journey, you will be too late. There's no take-out window or quick fix for an unexamined life.

That being said, it can take only moments to improve some things, and to right some wrongs. It's just the sooner you start, the further you can go. And why not go far?

PART 2

PRACTICE THROUGH EVERYDAY ATTITUDES, ACTIONS & REACTIONS

The following cartoons and practices contain the mindful concepts used by the author most often. Each is a gem in the art and practice of applied mindfulness.

ACCEPT

ACCEPT

SELF: People tend to see what they expect, so accepting "what is," separate from pre-conceived judgments is an important mindful practice. An initial attitude of curiosity or acceptance helps you absorb information with an open mind, so you don't react quickly out of habit, or due to assumptions.

RELATIONSHIPS: An attitude of mutual acceptance creates a trusting relationship where people don't always have to worry about being criticized or rejected. Different needs or opinions can be addressed without basic acceptance being revoked. People feel respected when their ideas and feelings are heard and understood, even when not agreed with.

PRACTICE: Intentionally go through your day with the goal of being more accepting about what you see, hear, and feel. Try to note "what is" without feeling the need to add your opinion or judgment, either out loud, or in your thoughts. Make room for the unknown and unexpected, by not always defaulting to your comfort zones.

SEE: Beginner's Mind p.160; Observing Actions & Reactions p.164; Practicing Non-Judgment p.169; Feeling Body Sensation & Movements p.170; Opening Heart & Mind p.174

ADAPT

ADAPT

SELF: Mindfulness helps people adapt -moment to moment- by helping them see more information through less biased eyes. People who find it hard to adapt may struggle with change, or fail to notice details about themselves or others due to judgments, fears, or attachment to habits. Mindfulness helps you become more flexible, so you can adapt and evolve over time.

RELATIONSHIPS: An adaptive person in relationships takes a position of openness instead of being rigid or inflexible. Adapting in relationships isn't about just doing what others want, it's about helping all parties contribute relevant information so more possibilities become apparent.

PRACTICE: Go into your day prepared to notice when you feel stuck, irritated, or insecure. Take note of your typical reaction, and try to replace it with telling yourself you are conflicted. Breathe slower and deeper and give yourself time to think about what the conflict is. Accept that the conflict exists, and instead of avoiding it or reacting out of habit, find an adaptive solution.

See: Working with Thoughts or Emotions p.162; Observing Actions & Reactions p.164; Practicing Non-Struggle p.166; Noticing or Deepening the Breath p.168

ANGER

ANGER

SELF: Anger is often a reaction to feeling vulnerable or hurt, but the vulnerability may be hidden beneath aggression, or not well understood. Before acting out in anger, a mindful practice is to ask what fear or vulnerable emotions triggered the anger. When you're aware of this, you can let yourself feel the vulnerable upset and try to work through it, instead of covering or compounding it with anger.

RELATIONSHIPS: It is okay to feel anger, but less okay to direct it at people. Directed anger is aggressive and therefore disrespectful. If you don't like to be disrespected, can you justify disrespecting someone else? If you're more mindful of anger when it begins in your thoughts, you can try to understand and resolve it before directing it at someone through words or actions. Problems can be talked through more easily with respectful patience, than with anger.

PRACTICE: Do everything thirty percent slower. Breathe, speak, eat, move, act, and react more slowly because it builds space into your mental and emotional reaction time. This releases tension that comes from the pressure to do things quickly, so you're less likely to react, or let frustration build through the day.

SEE: Working with Thoughts or Emotions p.162, Observing Actions & Reactions p.164, Softening the Hard Edges p.173

APPRECIATE

APPRECIATE

SELF: Appreciating things depends on being able to notice them in the first place. The mind lets you attend to information at a deep level, surface level, or you may ignore it altogether. Mindful practice brings more to see, feel, know, and appreciate onto the screen of your attention.

RELATIONSHIPS: Life and people are constantly evolving, so it makes more sense to approach interactions with curiosity, than to make assumptions based on how things went before. Watch your words and actions, and be more spontaneous instead of acting out of habit. When people are appreciated daily, it's easier for relationships to remain strong and supportive.

PRACTICE: Go into your day with a goal of noticing things you like. Many people are in the habit of thinking about what's wrong, instead of appreciating what's right. With this practice you might see dozens of things in one day which you've been forgetting to appreciate. Life must be appreciated in small moments, and not just "managed," or raced through, or one day you'll wonder where your life went.

See: Beginner's Mind p.160, Coming Back to the Present p.163, Dropping Busy Mind p.165, Feeling Empathy, Compassion, Gratitude p.167, Opening Heart & Mind p.174

ATTACHMENT

ATTACHMENT

SELF: Attachment to ideas, habits, wants, judgments, and routine keeps people from noticing and appreciating the present. If your mind is already convinced about how things are, or what has to happen, new possibilities can't get in. Try to bring curiosity into each moment because there might be something there for you that will be missed if expectations get in the way.

RELATIONSHIPS: The more attached people are to "the way things have to be," the harder they are to negotiate or reason with. This is a liability in relationships where different needs and feelings must be considered, respected, and managed.

PRACTICE: Spend a day observing the needs and problems you project onto others, in your thoughts, words, and actions. Observe them with this question in the background: "Is this the correct way to focus my attention?" Note the birthplace of your stronger needs and problems, and think about whether you're focusing on them in the most positive or constructive way. When imposing a requirement on someone, ask yourself if you would be okay if a similar thing was asked of you, in the same manner.

See: Beginner's Mind p.160, Practicing Non-Struggle p.166, Practicing Non-Judgment p.169, Feeling Body Sensation & Movements p.170, Opening Heart & Mind p.174

AVOIDANCE

...AND IF I SEE HIM COMING, I'M CROSSING THE STREET! SEE HOW HE LIKES THE COLD SHOULDER ROUTINE. I'M TALKING DEEP FREEZE CANADIAN WINTER COLD SHOULDER WITH NO SPRING IN SIGHT UNLESS...

IF YOU HAVE TO PUT EFFORT INTO AVOIDING SOMETHING, YOU'RE STILL CONNECTED. WHY NOT SOLVE THE PROBLEM AND BE FREE OF IT FOR REAL?

AVOIDANCE

SELF: People avoid the things they're afraid of facing directly. Mindful people let themselves notice their fear so they can try to understand it. After noticing and accepting fear, it's possible to do something constructive about it. Running from fear or pretending it's not there, keeps it alive, however ignored it is.

RELATIONSHIPS: Avoidance in relationships is a recipe for growing apart. Fear of facing problems or each other turns into avoidance, and more conflict is created by the avoidance itself. People with avoidant tendencies can let conflicts build to the point where they seem impossible to face or solve.

PRACTICE: When you catch yourself procrastinating, even when you really want to accomplish something, sit down and define the fears beneath your avoidance. People might spend years procrastinating for something as simple as restlessness, not knowing the next step in a process, or having problems with organization. If fears are defined, they can be broken down into solvable problems. When fears remain undefined, you keep working around them without knowing you're doing it, or why you make the decisions you do.

See: Working with Thoughts or Emotions p.162, Observing Actions & Reactions p.164, Practicing Non-Struggle p.166, Noticing the Space Around Things p.172

BENEVOLENCE

BENEVOLENCE

SELF: A benevolent attitude has goodwill and positive intentions behind it. People with a benevolent focus understand how to help themselves and others by coming from a place of love over hate, and generosity over greed. Those who see the value of helping others know we're all connected, and happiness is not something to compete for, but to share. True confidence comes from knowing you are a positive presence in the world, contributing something to "the good" with your unique presence and skills.

RELATIONSHIPS: A proactive, consciously benevolent attitude is necessary for people to be able to choose the loving act or response over the fearful/angry one when challenged. Benevolence is not only a possibility, but a responsibility if people expect to have and keep respectful, loving relationships.

PRACTICE: It's easy for people to fall into the trap of carrying out daily responsibilities without thinking about the attitude they are projecting into the world. Go through your day observing the energy or atmosphere you carry around with you. See if you can add in more softness, kindness, or benevolent intentions to your thoughts, words, and actions. Note how it feels and how others respond.

See: Observing Actions & Reactions p.164, Dropping Busy Mind p.165, Feeling Empathy, Compassion, Gratitude p.167, Softening the Hard Edges p.173

BREATHE

BREATHE

SELF: Noticing the breath is a key mindful practice. The breath is always there in the present moment, unlike the mind which can travel to the past or future while the present goes unnoticed. Coming back to the breath helps anchor people in the here and now so they can feel more in the present, and follow scattered-mind less often.

RELATIONSHIPS: If you find yourself in a challenging conversation, instead of reacting immediately, tune into your breath as you slow down your breathing. Get into the habit of feeling and hearing the breath when stressed, and let your slow relaxed breathing remind you there's no need to rush a response or reaction.

PRACTICE: Tune into your breath and feel your body as it moves in space (instead of thinking thoughts). When walking or doing menial tasks, give your brain a rest from repetitive thinking habits by using all your attention to feel your breath and body instead. This helps ground anxious energy, to the point where you can notice your body and mind relaxing. Also of great importance for longterm practice goals: each time you interrupt automatic thinking habits by focusing "on purpose," you build the capacity to focus and clear your mind at will.

See: Coming Back to the Present p.163, Dropping Busy Mind p.165, Noticing or Deepening the Breath p.168, Feeling Body Sensation & Movements p.170

CHOICE

The view from outside the box

IT'S EASY TO "BOX YOURSELF IN" AND THINK CHOICES ARE SIMILAR TO ONES YOU'VE MADE BEFORE. THE VIEW FROM OUTSIDE THE BOX IS MUCH MORE EXPANSIVE

CHOICE

SELF: In each moment, people have a choice about how to think, feel, and behave, but it's easy to slip into reactive mode and think you're doing things because you "have to." Mindful people make a point of challenging their assumptions when it seems like they don't have choices. Mindful practice changes your focus so you stop seeing yourself as a reactor in your own life, and you become the actor instead; the one who makes choices about what to think, feel, do, and believe.

RELATIONSHIPS: People often feel restricted by a perceived lack of choice. In relationships, this can cause you to be defensive, or feel "backed into a corner." People actually have many choices available to them in a given moment. It's a choice to listen, be respectful, and stay open to problem solving. Choose the more loving response over the automatic defensive one to keep relationships healthy and happy.

PRACTICE: People often let themselves remain stuck in the same behaviours, even when they're unhappy. Go into your day with the intention of noticing when you feel stressed, stuck, or bored, and spend some time thinking about why you feel like you do. Think in more detail about what you need and want, then make a new choice.

See: Beginner's Mind p.160, Working with Thoughts or Emotions p.162, Coming Back to the Present p.163

COMMUNICATE

FAILURE TO OPENLY COMMUNICATE
JAMS YOU UP WITH UNFINISHED BUSINESS

COMMUNICATE

SELF: The only way we can be known is through communication. Good communicators can define needs, feelings, and ideas, and share them with others. They're also able to listen while others do the same. If communication is consistently difficult, it's often because people resort to trading reactive signals. All your important communication should be out loud (not body language, or 'mind reading'), honest, fair, specific, relevant, and to the point, rather than suggestive, general, passive aggressive, or based on assumptions.

RELATIONSHIPS: Good communicators know how to use words, and they're also empathetic and fair. Healthy communication respects others and lacks aggression or threat, either spoken or unspoken. People who fail to communicate well may resort to aggression or avoidance due to frustration. Be more respectful and honest about feelings, while eliminating tensions caused by aggressive or avoidant behaviour.

PRACTICE: Approach communications for the day with an intention to break out of your habits. Find different questions to ask, different expressions, humour, and share stories that forge new territory, with a goal of creating meaningful connections (emotional intimacy).

See Beginner's Mind p.160, Coming Back to the Present p.163, Observing Actions & Reactions p.164, Practicing Non-Judgment p.169

CONFIDENT

WHEN YOU HAVE REAL CONFIDENCE, YOU
DON'T NEED LIMITED VIEWS AS PROTECTION

CONFIDENT

SELF: True confidence comes from self-understanding. Confidence can't be gathered up in the material world; it comes from taking detailed responsibility for the mental, emotional, physical and spiritual self. Non-integrated aspects of the self create insecurity and conflict. For example: mental or behavioural habits that don't line up with values and goals.

RELATIONSHIPS: Confident people don't gain power or self-congratulations by taking from others in either passive or aggressive ways. Truly confident people always face themselves and others with honesty and respect, and have a firm base of ethical attitudes and behaviour to stand on. A confident person is not threatened by the confidence of others.

PRACTICE: Go into your day and notice when you don't make eye contact or when you avoid people in other ways. Notice when you assume the worst, are dishonest, have negative self-talk, or criticize others (in thoughts or words). Ask yourself why any of these things are going on, and whether you have insecurities driving this behaviour. Then make a point of understanding and resolving insecurities (by facing fears), rather than using habits or defensive behaviours to cover them.

See: Feeling Open & Relaxed p.161, Working with Thoughts or Emotions p.162, Observing Actions & Reactions p.164, Dropping Busy Mind p.165, Softening the Hard Edges p.173

CONNECT

EVERY POSITIVE CONNECTION CAN BECOME PART OF
ANOTHER ONE THAT'S PASSED TO SOMEONE ELSE

CONNECT

SELF: Individual people seem quite separate from each other and the environment, but the world is composed of intermingled matter and energy. Vegetables you eat are fed by earth, sun and rain, and they become part of your blood and body. Plants give off oxygen, and we all breathe it in and out. People who feel your influence take it into their lives and are changed by it, as are the people connected to them.

RELATIONSHIPS: Personal responsibility extends beyond yourself to the people who are influenced by what you think, feel, and do. Like a rock creates ripples in water, energies ripple out from you to interact with others and the environment. A tiny positive thought or act sent out via the ripple effect could eventually help someone do great things.

PRACTICE: Make a point of thinking about the types of people you easily connect to. Why are these people in your comfort zone? Do they appreciate you? do they encourage and support you? Do you do the same for them? Could you be connecting to other types of people you'd like to meet if you did something different in your thoughts, actions, or reactions? Try an experiment in real life, and note the results.

See: Feeling Empathy, Compassion, Gratitude p.167, Practicing Non-Judgment p.169, Feeling Body Sensation & Movements p.170, Noticing the Space Around Things p.172

COURAGE

A MINDFUL PERSON COURAGEOUSLY DROPS BOMBS OF PEACE AND CLARITY ON A BUSY, DISTRACTED WORLD

COURAGE

SELF: People need courage to be able to face fear and change. Courage is the willingness to put yourself forward in faith without knowing how things will turn out. Courageous people know that ignoring the possibility of success is more painful than any failure. To muster more courage, resolve to treat failure as a learning experience. At the end of life, the pain of failure pales when compared to regret for not following your heart.

RELATIONSHIPS: In relationships, courage is often about things that are easy to overlook or undervalue. It's not a small thing to be willing to forgive; go the extra mile; perform selfless acts; admit mistakes; or expose vulnerabilities. These things are necessary for love to ignite and then fully thrive. People who are courageous enough to take emotional risks get to experience the most love as they get to know and love others.

PRACTICE: Identify a way in which you hold back emotionally in relationships. Choose something specific to be more open about, and wait for a good opportunity to apply your strategy. Note how it feels before and after. Work at becoming more relaxed over time with emotional honesty.

See: Working with Thoughts or Emotions p.162, Practicing Non-Struggle p.166, Feeling Empathy, Compassion, Gratitude p.167, Noticing the Space Around Things p. 172, Opening Heart & Mind p.174

DISCERNMENT

A ROUTINE CAN BE HELPFUL, OR IT CAN BE A
BUNCH OF HABITS THAT KEEP YOU PRISONER

DISCERNMENT

SELF: People are discerning when they're able to clearly see and weigh all relevant variables of a given problem. Wise people have discerning minds that are able to cut through extraneous information and get to the heart of an issue. Discernment is a skill developed by observing the world, yourself, and others to understand concepts, feelings, behaviour and motives (and how they all fit together).

RELATIONSHIPS: When people reflect enough to be aware of the roots of their own behaviours, they can be more discerning about the behaviour and needs of others. A discerning person can bring more quality and less confusion to relationships. Discerning people know when to speak or listen, plan or act; let things be or request an explanation.

PRACTICE: Go into your week with the intention to ask more questions and also to explain yourself more fully (to both yourself and others). See if you can add more interesting detail during an interaction, or if you can get others to do the same by asking relevant questions. Observe the motives behind your words and actions as if you were a character you were watching in a movie. What do you notice about yourself? Aim for kindness, respect, and authenticity.

See: Coming Back to the Present Moment p.163, Observing Actions & Reactions p.164, Noticing or Deepening the Breath p.168, Practicing Non-Judgment p.169, Noticing Sound, Colour, or Shapes p.171

DISCIPLINE

A MINDFUL LIFE IS A DISCIPLINE OF HAVING AND NOTICING
MOMENTS THAT ADD UP TO A LIFE YOU WERE GLAD TO HAVE

DISCIPLINE

SELF: Discipline helps people find more satisfaction in both work and leisure. An undisciplined mind may have trouble focusing on what matters, and contribute to a distracted, unsatisfying way of life. People who avoid discipline may often feel scattered and like work is never really finished. It takes practice feeling what is good about discipline -in each moment- before it seems easy and satisfying.

RELATIONSHIPS: Find a way to bring yourself to relationships so they can evolve and thrive over time. It's a discipline to continue to check in with others to ensure relationships stay positive and mutually beneficial. A relationship needs ongoing attention and disciplined action in order to grow.

PRACTICE: Beware of constantly chasing goals, only to miss living in the present moment. Mindful discipline means living everyday life in a way you've consciously chosen. Move toward your goals in a disciplined way, but practice breathing and being fully present as you do one thing, and then one thing, with patient intention. This is a pleasant alternative to having an undisciplined or driven mind that rushes through things just to get to the end.

See: Coming Back to the Present Moment p.163, Dropping Busy Mind p.165, Practicing Non-Struggle p.166, Feeling Body Sensations & Movements p.170

DISTRACTED

IF YOU ASK SOMEONE A QUESTION THEN FORGET TO LISTEN TO THE ANSWER, DID YOU ACTUALLY ASK THE QUESTION TO BEGIN WITH, OR WAS IT ALL A DREAM?

DISTRACTED

SELF: The attention of distracted people is guided by random thoughts, habits, and outside stimulus rather than conscious choice. This is the equivalent of signing over personal choice and freedom. Mindful people use focusing practices to help them minimize distractions and thinking habits that don't add value to life. When your mind is clear, it can be used as an effective tool, or a refuge to experience peace.

RELATIONSHIPS: A distracted person has trouble being present when you want to engage. In a relationship this can feel like anything from lack of interest to abandonment. Children or spouses, for example, can be deeply hurt if they only get distracted attention. It feels like there's always something you'd rather be doing, or someone you'd rather be with. This may not be the case, you might just be busy or stressed. Be present in the moment you're in; it's good for you and everyone around you.

PRACTICE: Commit to focusing on one thing at a time, all day, while following your slow deep breathing in the background. Even if you're multi-tasking, you can really only do one thing, then one thing. For example, pick up the pen, look to the left, open the file, begin reading, stop to ask the kids to be quiet, re-focus on reading...while breathing. Stay aware of relaxed hands, feet and shoulders.

See: Coming Back to the Present Moment p.163, Dropping Busy Mind p.165, Practicing Non-Struggle p.166, Noticing or Deepening the Breath p.168

EMPATHY

EMPATHY

SELF: An empathetic person can identify and understand how others feel. To develop more empathy, spend time observing yourself and others, and be more honest and open about feelings. Empathy creates deeper meaning and intimacy in relationships, and it helps people comprehend the subtleties that drive others. Empathy is a bridge that people's needs and feelings meet on to be fully understood and engaged with.

RELATIONSHIPS: Empathetic people can step outside their own egos and see others as individuals, who are not just extensions of their own needs or concerns. Mindfulness practice can help you learn to empathize more by reducing the tension in your mind, body, and emotions. It's easier to notice and care about others when you're not always fielding conflict in your own thoughts and feelings.

PRACTICE: Go into your day with the intention of tuning into different people's feelings, by taking a "feeling snapshot" of what they might be going through in a particular moment. Consider what they're doing, their needs/wants, and their history. If you don't know them very well, imagine what their needs, wants, and history might be. Speak with them to confirm your predictions, when possible or appropriate.

See: Feeling Empathy, Compassion, Gratitude p.167, Practicing Non-Judgment p.169, Opening Heart & Mind p.174

EQUANIMITY

EQUANIMITY EXEMPTS YOU FROM THE NEVER-ENDING
TUG OF WAR BETWEEN DESIRE AND DISPLEASURE

EQUANIMITY

SELF: Equanimity is an attitude that helps you respond to all kinds of experience with grace. If you divide life into strong categories of good and bad, you can fall into a habit of not accepting many things. Both pleasant and unpleasant things happen, whether you accept them or not. Much suffering is caused by struggling against problems or discomfort, instead of focusing on the best way to manage whatever comes.

RELATIONSHIPS: If you face relationship conflicts with an attitude of equanimity, you can stay calm enough to let facts and feelings present themselves before you act or react. Equanimity helps you struggle less over the particulars of how things happen, so many unnecessary conflicts can be prevented. An equanimous outlook can help you notice, and then resolve, competitive reactions and thinking habits.

PRACTICE: Try to go through a whole day without becoming outwardly irritated with anything or anybody. Then try to go a whole day without even becoming inwardly irritated. Continue to lengthen the time of your practice, while addressing the underlying judgments, habits, and other attachments that feed irritability and cause you to react with negativity or frustration when things don't go your way.

See: Beginner's Mind p.160, Feeling Open & Relaxed p.161, Observing Actions & Reactions p.164, Practicing Non-Struggle p.166, Practicing Non-Judgment p.169

FEAR

IF YOU CATCH YOURSELF OVERREACTING, OR AVOIDING
SOMETHING, SEE IF THERE'S FEAR AT THE BOTTOM OF IT

FEAR

SELF: Negative or rigid attitudes and reactions are mostly driven by fear, and it's a mindful practice to notice this. If you had no fear you wouldn't need protective defenses like anger, perfectionism, or avoidance. Fearful responses lack mindfulness because they're reactive instead of proactive. Nobody decides to be angry, anxious, or avoidant on purpose, these are reactions to feeling vulnerable. Ask yourself what those vulnerabilities are, and attend to them with care.

RELATIONSHIPS: In relationships, people fear being hurt so they defend themselves in different ways. People's fears, and the defenses they build around them, cause destructive conflicts in relationships. If people weren't afraid, they'd have no reason to overreact, or avoid relationship issues. Eliminate fear and defense, and require yourself and others to work through problems using calm communication and mutual respect.

PRACTICE: For a whole week, if you notice you're avoiding something or overreacting, ask yourself: What are the underlying fears? Let yourself feel the fear and any related vulnerable emotions, then replace avoidance or overreactions with problem-solving. You are strong enough to face your feelings.

See: Feeling Open & Relaxed p.161, Working With Thoughts or Emotions p.162, Observing Actions & Reactions p.164, Practicing Non-Struggle p.166, Softening the Hard Edges p.173

FOCUS

FOCUS

SELF: A focused mind can achieve more because it can direct its resources where they're needed, and away from unwanted experience or distractions. The ability to focus is required for in-depth thinking and also for clearing the mind at will. You can clear the mind when you train it to focus away from unintentional thoughts, or habits that keep it constantly roaming.

RELATIONSHIPS: A person who can focus stays more present with you in the moment to listen, respond, and experience things together. Mindfulness can help keep relationships running smoothly because it's a practice of noticing all important issues that cross the mind and the moment, so they can be tended to.

PRACTICE: The ability to focus can be built through training, by using focusing practices. Challenge yourself to focus on what you hear, and on feeling your breath go in and out, instead of focusing on thoughts. Try it for the entire length of a walk or a drive, or while stretching or watching a movie. When you default back to focusing on thoughts, just notice and then bring your attention back to the breath and what you hear.

See: Coming Back to the Present Moment p.163, Dropping Busy Mind p.165, Noticing or Deepening the Breath p.168, Feeling Body Sensation & Movements p.170, Noticing the Space Around Things p.172

FORGIVE

FORGIVE

SELF: If you don't let go of a hurtful situation, your energy stays attached to it via thoughts and feelings. Forgiveness is about healing, not condoning bad behaviour. Only you can take control of your power and focus. Mindful people try not to feel like anyone's victim even when they're treated poorly. To be a victim means someone has power over you, but those who harm others do it out of weakness or ignorance, not strength. It can help to remember this.

RELATIONSHIPS: Forgiveness is difficult when people won't admit wrongdoing. Asking for forgiveness helps a hurt party feel understood and cared for, and it releases both sides of a conflict from tension and negativity. Whether or not a mature resolution is reached, forgiveness can be found within oneself, to help release negative energy and resentment. Create stronger boundaries between yourself and those who don't show you basic respect.

PRACTICE: Think about the people you have not forgiven. Reflect on the reasons for holding onto resentment and try to feel and resolve the associated emotions. Forgiveness often happens in stages as you free yourself gradually from stuck or painful emotions.

See: Beginner's Mind p.160, Working with Thoughts or Emotions p.162, Observing Actions & Reactions p.164, Practicing Non-Struggle p.166, Opening Heart & Mind p.174

FREEDOM

FREEDOM

SELF: Mindfulness practice brings people closer to freedom with each space in the mind that is cleared of distraction or conflict. What's in your mind affects everything you feel and do, so more consciously chosen thoughts equals more choice and freedom in life. Unconscious habits usurp your freedom every time you have an automatic thought or reaction that stands in the way of more constructive thoughts that could create better outcomes.

RELATIONSHIPS: A relationship where people feel free but connected at the same time depends on always coming back to a place of understanding. This means addressing conflict as you go, and not letting confusion build. If people get lost in compounded conflicts, they're always focused on problems instead of the good things in life and relationships. This has the potential to eclipse freedom and quality of life considerably.

PRACTICE: Next time your family member says something that irritates you, continue to listen and be calm, as if you have all the time in the world for them to explain their thinking, without your input. It's freeing to release yourself from the need to approve or disapprove all the time. People are responsible for their own opinions, and sometimes they're more likely to hear problems with their logic or tone if you're not talking.

See Beginner's Mind p.160, Coming Back to the Present p.163, Practicing Non-Struggle p.166, Practicing Non-Judgment p.169

HONESTY

HONESTY

SELF: Your level of honesty with others depends on how honest you are with yourself. Your mind can easily hide aspects of your own reality unless you self-reflect and honestly face what you see. The more detail you understand about your mental, emotional and physical behaviour, the more you can "keep yourself honest."

RELATIONSHIPS: Beneath dishonesty are fears and aspects of character that haven't been examined or resolved. Where lying is avoidant, honesty shows a willingness to face yourself and others directly. People should feel safe to be open and honest in close relationships, and if not, they should examine issues with trust, fear, empathy and integrity.

PRACTICE: Notice if you catch yourself being dishonest in any form, whether it's sparing someone's feelings, lying without reason, or outright manipulation. Take a good look at the motives behind any dishonest interactions. Challenge yourself to align motives and behaviour with values you feel good about. If you're unsure about your motives, ask yourself how you'd feel if someone was dishonest with you in the same way, and if you would have preferred some other way of being dealt with.

See: Working with Thoughts or Emotions p.162, Observing Actions & Reactions p.164, Practicing Non-Judgment p.169

HUMILITY

HUMILITY

SELF: Truly humble people don't think others are above or beneath them because they don't buy into superficial status. They know only insecure people display arrogance or the need to position themselves above others. If you're humble you know another's hardship could easily be your own given the same circumstances.

RELATIONSHIPS: People show humility when they take down defenses and engage with others openly, as equals. This kind of cooperative behaviour shows respect instead of the fear and aggression that's evident when people compete or avoid each other. It shows humility when you try to understand people instead of passing judgment. Humility is a simple and humble formula for creating high quality relationships.

PRACTICE: Next time you overreact, ask yourself how your needs or standards became so inflated in your mind as to justify an overreaction. Is there anything about the concept of your position or importance that's bothering you, or are you being affected by unresolved conflicts?

See: Working with Thoughts or Emotions p.162, Observing Actions & Reactions p.164, Feeling Empathy, Compassion, Gratitude p.167, Opening Heart & Mind p.174

IGNORANCE

IF YOU FEEL STUCK OR RESTLESS, NOTICE IF YOU'RE ACTING OUT
OF HABIT INSTEAD OF MAKING CONSCIOUS DECISIONS.

IGNORANCE

SELF: Everyone has aspects of character that can be improved through more awareness, understanding, or education. Ignorance of many subjects is unavoidable, but it needn't be a defining part of your character if your mind and communication stays open. A mindful approach to life assumes there is always more you could learn, so bring curiosity to each moment instead of closing down out of habit, ignorance, or fear.

RELATIONSHIPS: In relationships, ignorance often shuts down communication or fair exchange. Ignorant behaviour is both defensive and offensive, so it seems aggressive, but is really based in fear. Think about what the fears are, and engage more fully to solve problems instead of "making them go away" with aggressive or avoidant power plays. Ignorance prevents you from knowing both yourself and others.

PRACTICE: The next time you are astounded by a loved one's ignorance, remind yourself of a time when you were ignorant about something and were harshly corrected. Think about a more compassionate way to discuss the issue, without using shame, anger, or arrogance.

See: Working with Thoughts or Emotions p.162, Observing Actions & Reactions p.164, Feeling Empathy, Compassion, Gratitude p.167, Noticing or Deepening the Breath p.168, Practicing Non-Judgment p.169

IMPERMANENCE

NOT SO LONG AS YOU MIGHT THINK

15   30   45   60   75

time (yrs)

WHEN YOU'RE TALKING TO PEOPLE, PICTURE THEM AS CHILDREN, ADULTS, AND IN THEIR OLD AGE. DOES IT CHANGE ANYTHING?

IMPERMANENCE

SELF: Many people focus a lot of attention into building permanent security. This seems like a smart goal, but it doesn't account for the impermanent nature of life. Grasping at security, permanence, and predictability in an ever-changing world causes a lot of unnecessary suffering. Mindfulness helps people engage more fully in the present moment to learn how to find truth, value, and security there. Be responsible and discerning about security issues, but not controlling, fearful, or inflexible.

RELATIONSHIPS: If people keep in mind how short life is, and how impermanent relationships really are, they don't as easily harm or disrespect others. A tendency to lash out at a family member, friend, or stranger, is partly based on the false idea that there's always time to make up, or right wrongs. People's feelings and life as a whole are not games to be carelessly played with. Many people reach the end of life with painful regrets about their careless treatment of others.

PRACTICE: Picture yourself in the moments before your own death. Think about how you will have to live, so that moment will find you at peace, rather than feeling regret. Learn to contemplate and accept the circle of life.

See: Beginner's Mind p.160, Coming Back to the Present p.163, Practicing Non-Struggle p.166, Noticing the Space Around Things p.172, Softening the Hard Edges p.173

INSPIRE

INSPIRE

SELF: People need role models, and they are role models to those around them. Who inspires you, and what do you inspire in others? Many people feel alone in the world, but this is an illusion. There is vast life around you, and plenty of inspiration if you learn how to access it through nature, ideas, art, creativity, education, and people. Inspire others with your unique abilities, find what inspires you, and take part in the give and take network all around you.

RELATIONSHIPS: We live in a cause and effect world, so it's important to notice how everything you do affects your life and those around you. In relationships it's easy to get into the habit of discouraging what you don't want instead of inspiring something good. Inspiration supports people while criticism brings them down. Mutual inspiration helps relationships stay exciting, and retain the magic feeling that comes from supportive love and attention.

PRACTICE: Think about a goal that you can get very excited about. Work out the smaller steps you will have to take to meet your goal. Think in detail about what it would be like if you actually accomplished your goal. If this doesn't inspire you, think more about what you really want, or about fears connected to getting what you want.

See: Beginner's Mind p.160, Coming Back to the Present Moment p.163, Observing Actions & Reactions p.164, Opening Heart & Mind p.174

INTEGRITY

IF SOMEONE GETS SNARKY WITH YOU, DOES IT EVER
SEEM JUSTIFIED, LIKE WHEN YOU DO IT TO OTHERS?

INTEGRITY

SELF: People with integrity make a conscious effort to align thoughts, words, and actions with their values. Instead of imposing standards on others, make a point of upholding them yourself. Mindful people hold even their thoughts to a level of integrity, because they know words, tone, feelings, actions, and inactions begin as thoughts.

RELATIONSHIPS: It's important to maintain your integrity, no matter what other people are doing. You're in charge of you. It's easy to become confused about boundaries and responsibilities in relationships, so it's an ongoing mindful practice to maintain personal integrity when you're being challenged by others.

PRACTICE: Think about all the things you want to be included in your daily life. Are these things currently in your life, or do you need to make adjustments over time? Take a specific period of time to focus on how you spend your days, to see if it matches up with values you believe in. Cultivate the ability to tolerate uncertainty if you're unsure about how to make changes. For every problem there is a solution.

See: Observing Actions & Reactions p.164, Dropping Busy Mind p.165, Practicing Non-Judgment p.169, Feeling Body Sensations & Movements p.170, Noticing the Space Around Things p.172, Opening Heart & Mind p.174

JUDGMENT

JUDGMENT

SELF: When people over-focus on "what's wrong," they can fail to see or look for what's right. What is right (or possible) is there, whether you look for it or not. Critics with rigid attitudes and judgments don't realize how often they shut themselves off from seeing the good in things. People that belittle others through judgment and criticism get a false sense of security from putting themselves "in the right."

RELATIONSHIPS: When people in relationships judge each other, they're competing instead of cooperating. Little can be gained from launching accusations back and forth, and it can even cause irreparable damage. Respectful sharing of thoughts, feelings, and potential solutions can heal problems in a way that trading judgments cannot. The tendency to judge harshly is rooted in lack of integrity, competition, and stereotyping.

PRACTICE: Next time you notice yourself harshly judging or criticizing, ask yourself what fear, frustration, or insecurity is the cause (because why not speak and act with consideration and empathy)? Work on resolving and understanding hurt feelings, instead of projecting them onto others.

See Beginner's Mind p.160, Working with Thoughts or Emotions p.162, Feeling Empathy, Compassion, Gratitude p.167, Practicing Non-Judgment p.169, Softening the Hard Edges p.173

LOVE

LOVE

SELF: In each situation, in every moment, there's a choice between taking a loving or not so loving approach. The key is to take responsibility for the attitude you choose. A personal commitment to being a positive, ethical, loving person is what it takes to give and receive the most love. Mindful people take responsibility for the degree of love in their own thoughts, words, and actions, and don't only focus on how they're being treated or responded to.

RELATIONSHIPS: It takes a conscious decision to choose the loving thought, word, or action when challenged. This is why love is an ongoing mindful practice. When you're tempted to behave in an unloving way, don't do it until you've asked yourself what you'd do or how you'd feel if someone did the same to you. Before long, a practice like this makes it clear that everyone's good is served (yours included) by choosing the more loving action.

PRACTICE: Proactively choose to make a loving gesture toward someone in your life. Then, keep up the practice of loving "on purpose" and see if you notice any shifts in your relationships.

See: Beginner's Mind p.160, Coming Back to the Present p.163, Feeling Empathy, Compassion, Gratitude p.167, Noticing the Space Around Things p.172, Opening Heart & Mind p.174

MAGNANIMOUS

MAGNANIMOUS

SELF: Magnanimous people are willing to forgive an injustice, and give more in the face of receiving less. When you're magnanimous you strive to be the bigger person rather than holding a grudge or being resentful when someone's treatment of you is less than perfect. All kinds of generosity are possible when you realize some people have less to give, and it's often because less was given to them.

RELATIONSHIPS: People who have enough humility to suspend judgment and give others the benefit of the doubt, make room for discussion and solution. They also take into account the reality that people aren't perfect, and someone's mistake, bad day, or personality problem isn't always an attack that warrants defending.

PRACTICE: The next time someone gets snippy with you, don't snap back. Breathe, and remain calm and casual. If they're expecting you to snap back, but only get a calm presence and understanding in return, they will be more likely to think about what they've done and apologize, or do better next time. Sometimes making room for imperfection is an expression of love, consideration, or trust that earns you more trust in return.

See: Beginner's Mind p.160, Observing Actions and Reactions p.164, Practicing Non-Judgment p.169, Softening the Hard Edges p.173, Opening Heart & Mind p.174

OBSERVE

OBSERVE

SELF: A mindful person cultivates the ability to be a detached observer. As an observer you try to "see what is" separate from emotion, judgments, and other biases that cloud perception. An observer lifts the screen of ego, or personal interests and habits, to look at what happens. The goal is to separate expectations or pre-conceived ideas from what is happening in the present moment.

RELATIONSHIPS: The habits and trends of a relationship can be observed as a system that both parties create and uphold. From this less personal perspective, it's easier to see what happens and why, when things go wrong. Relationships are multi-person systems, so if things are only seen and judged from one person's viewpoint, information can be skewed and confusing because it's inaccurate. In relationships there are always different perspectives to consider.

PRACTICE: Observe how you feel first thing in the morning, before you get out of bed. What needs to happen to your feelings, mood, health, activities, or beliefs (if anything), for you to feel excited about starting the day, every day?

See: Beginner's Mind p.160, Coming Back to the Present p.163, Noticing or Deepening the Breath p.168, Practicing Non-Judgment p.169, Noticing Sound, Colour, or Shapes p.171, Noticing the Space Around Things p.172

OPTIMISM

OPTIMISM

SELF: When you observe your train of thought, you'll notice a prevailing trend of either optimism or pessimism. Optimism acts like a filter to show you positive aspects of people and situations, and pessimism does the opposite. An optimist and a pessimist living through the same day would therefore experience different things because one is focused on what's right, and the other is focused on what's wrong.

RELATIONSHIPS: Pessimists don't take enough responsibility for how they affect themselves or others with their attitudes and choices. They don't see the good, and don't seem willing to look for it. Both people in a relationship are responsible for its quality, and for helping it evolve, so this is where being around a pessimist equals too much take and not enough give. When you can't find the good in things, how is it possible to evolve, improve, or enjoy life as it happens?

PRACTICE: Think about your most cherished dream or goal, and how to work with it in your real life, not just in thoughts. Use optimism and vision to build and follow concrete steps to your goal. Climb them one step, one breath at a time.

See: Beginner's Mind p.160, Coming Back to the Present p.163, Practicing Non-Struggle p.166, Noticing or Deepening the Breath p.168

PATIENCE

THE MOMENT IMPATIENCE ARRIVES,
MINDFULNESS GOES OUT THE WINDOW

PATIENCE

SELF: Impatience is the product of not settling into the moment you're in. When people are calm enough to be present in the moment, they can see and feel what's good about being there and appreciate it. If you're too anxious, restless or agitated, explore the reasons why, and do practices to calm your thoughts, emotions, and physical tension. Skimming over the surface of life's moments, or always passing over the now for what's next results in a lifetime being passed over eventually.

RELATIONSHIPS: Impatient people over-focus on the future and under-focus on the present. They can rob relationships of quality interactions and experience by never having the time or focus to "be here now." Impatient people resist or ignore "what is" while looking for an imaginary or not yet present "what may be." In relationships, this can read as not being there for people, or ignoring the things that matter most.

PRACTICE: Patiently explore what you already have for a period of time, and notice when (and why) your thoughts wander away from "what is" to "what's next." Make sure you move toward things with conscious intention and sound values, rather than impatience.

See: Coming Back to the Present p.163, Dropping Busy Mind p.165, Practicing Non-Struggle p.166, Noticing or Deepening the Breath p.168

PERSPECTIVE

PERSPECTIVE

SELF: It helps you keep things in proper perspective if you pay attention to how life as a whole and the present moment are related. If you stay mindful of the overall life you want to live, it's easier to make wise choices moment to moment. People can lose perspective when they forget that "the little things" are key to a high quality of life.

RELATIONSHIPS: When a relationship is approached with the perspective of fostering ongoing growth, it prevents you from getting stuck in bad habits. Life is dynamic and always changing. Relationships need to be as well to benefit participants on an ongoing basis. A simple perspective in relationships is to have a goal like trying to add to each other's lives without taking things away.

PRACTICE: If you add up enough mindless days, you come to the end of life without having lived yet. Each moment and each interaction can be useful or meaningful, if you approach it from a mindful perspective. Go through the day with the background thought that everything you do and say has meaning, and notice where you could adjust your behaviour so this truth is acknowledged.

See: Beginner's Mind p.160, Working with Thoughts or Emotions p.162, Noticing or Deepening the Breath p.168, Opening Heart & Mind p.174

PRESENCE

FIND MORE SPACE TO PATIENTLY LOOK AROUND.
THE MOMENT MIGHT BE LOOKING BACK AT YOU.

PRESENCE

SELF: While people chase threads of thoughts and feelings through their minds, they can miss noticing what happens in the present moment. Mindful practice helps you notice and address conflicted, scattered, or racing thoughts, so you can use your mind more intentionally now. And now... And now...

RELATIONSHIPS: The more present you are, the more you can participate in relationships. A person could be physically present, but absent on the mental-emotional fronts. Being more present on all levels means deeper connection, meaning and intimacy is possible in relationships.

PRACTICE: If you focus on how your body feels as you move, it can help you stay present, relaxed, and out of busy thoughts. Feel your feet on the ground and what you touch. Follow your breath going in and out, relax on the out-breath, and rest content in the moment you're in, one movement, one breath at a time. If your body is tight or stressed, try stretching, exercise, and increasing the length of your in-breath to see if you can "loosen up" over time.

See: Working with Thoughts or Emotions p.162, Coming Back to the Present p.163, Dropping Busy Mind p.165, Noticing or Deepening the Breath p.168, Feeling Body Sensation & Movements p.170, Noticing Sound, Colour, or Shapes p.171

RECONCILE

PROBLEMS COME TO YOUR HOUSE TO LOOK FOR CRACKS IN YOUR FOUNDATION. BEST TO SHAKE HANDS AND SEE WHAT THEY WANT BEFORE THEY DO A FULL SEARCH OF THE HOUSE

RECONCILE

SELF: Reconciliation is about restoring harmony, or settling something that has become unsettled. In mindfulness practice, reconciliation begins in your thoughts, with any struggles that present there. Notice a struggle, and accept it's there without judging it, then work through each aspect of the problem without resisting it. Many people live with ongoing conflict because instead of working out details of solutions, they react against the problem.

RELATIONSHIPS: In relationships, points of contention must be settled or reconciled for trust to remain high. A build-up of conflicts affects the integrity of a relationship and exacerbates other problems. Reconciliation is an ongoing practice that's about restoring peace, trust, and relationship security, so perpetual conflict doesn't become what your relationship is about.

PRACTICE: Think about any unfinished business you have, or conflicts that remain unresolved. What can you do from your side to find resolution, within yourself and/or with others? Be willing to explicitly apologize for your part in things, regardless of what others do. Reconciling doesn't always depend on the other person's reaction, it's about doing what you believe in, and getting right with your conscience.

See Working with Thoughts or Emotions p.162; Observing Actions and Reactions p.164; Practicing Non-Struggle p.166; Feeling Empathy, Compassion, Gratitude p.167

REFLECT

IF YOU DON'T REFLECT ON YOUR THOUGHTS AND
FEELINGS IT'S HARD TO KNOW WHAT TO DO WITH THEM

REFLECT

SELF: To evolve as a person, reflect on what motivates thoughts, feelings, and behaviour. It's only possible to learn from mistakes or adjust to change, if you're aware of yourself and what you're doing to begin with. Mindful people reflect on feelings and reactions, in good times, and during upsetting times or conflict, in order to fully experience and understand life as it happens.

RELATIONSHIPS: In relationships people often act or react before reflecting to understand what exactly they're reacting to. For example, if you feel bad, you may think your reaction is justified, no matter how irrational or unhelpful it is. The missing step is reflecting to see why something upset you so much you had to react. Why be reactive instead of just doing what's needed to respond calmly or solve the problem? (Answer: because you're feeling vulnerable. Identify the fear or vulnerability beneath your overreaction, and work to resolve it).

PRACTICE: Reflect on your life as a whole. What kinds of situations or relationships keep coming up? Is there something you could do to adjust your patterns or achieve more positive outcomes?

See: Feeling Open & Relaxed p.161, Working with Thoughts or Emotions p.162, Observing Actions & Reactions p.164, Noticing or Deepening the Breath p.168; Practicing Non-Judgment p.169

RESENTMENT

PRESSURE FROM UNEXPRESSED SADNESS CAUSES
THE DISCOMFORT THAT COMES WITH RESENTMENT

RESENTMENT

SELF: When resentment arises, you have emotions to work through. Allowing yourself to stew in resentment means you're not addressing the underlying emotional conflict. Drop your guard, let go of feeling aggressive, and let your vulnerable emotions come through. When you allow yourself to feel sadness, fear, or disappointment, the pain from that can be understood and resolved inwardly, if not always with others.

RELATIONSHIPS: You focus on resentment when you think of yourself as a victim and someone or something as your oppressor. Dwelling on resentment is not helpful, but working through feelings and solutions is. Resentment is not constructive because there's no solution in it. Negotiate change, accept that other people can't always be what you want them to be, and resolve feelings until you can move forward in peace.

PRACTICE: Decide if you need to communicate about anything in order to work through resentment. Notice how resentment feels in your body and mind, and resolve to clear it out so new healthy energy can come in. Cultivate satisfying relationships using the time and brain-space where nursing resentments used to be.

See: Working with Thoughts or Emotions p.162, Observing Actions & Reactions p.164, Feeling Empathy, Compassion, Gratitude p.167, Practicing Non-Judgment p.169

RESILIENCE

RESILIENT PEOPLE BELIEVE THERE'S A SOLUTION FOR EVERY
PROBLEM, AND IT'S A MATTER OF LETTING IT COME TO YOU

RESILIENCE

SELF: Resilience is the ability to weather conflict and hardships. Resilient people have optimistic outlooks and they invest in solutions over defeatist thinking. Emotional resilience points to good mental health and emotional maturity because it requires coping skills and adaptive strategies.

RELATIONSHIPS: In a relationship, you're resilient if you can be relied on to handle issues without shutting down. Mental resilience is shown by using the mind to optimize choice and experience. Emotional resilience means staying open to your own and others' feelings to work through them, even when it's difficult. People shut down or lose resilience when they feel overwhelmed or afraid, and become reactive instead of appropriately responsive. Resilience isn't about allowing or putting up with poor treatment, it takes two to maintain respect and caring in a relationship, through mindful attention.

PRACTICE: Next time you feel your willpower or confidence flagging, reflect on what you can do to bolster your resilience. What do you need to support yourself as you work through an issue? Do you need inspiration, self-care, support from others, education on a particular issue, or just a snack and a nap?

See: Beginner's Mind p.160, Coming Back to the Present p.163, Practicing Non-Struggle p.166, Opening Heart & Mind p.174

RESPECT

RESPECT

SELF: The foundation for respect toward others is respect for yourself. The things people fear and avoid in themselves create blindspots that prevent them from understanding and respecting others. When disrespect is present it's also due to stereotyping, or failing to see people as thinking, feeling, complex individuals.

RELATIONSHIPS: In close relationships, maintaining respect depends on people feeling considered and understood. Listening to others and good communication skills can build understanding and respect. People in relationships often get caught in a reactive loop where one person feels disrespected, and then feels justified to be disrespectful in return. Maintain personal integrity at all times to encourage respect from others, and more self-respect from within.

PRACTICE: When you notice yourself disrespecting or judging someone unfairly, remind yourself others are neither above nor below you, but equal, and that you can't fully understand everyone's history or why they've become who they are. Empathy and compassion both for yourself and others can heal a tendency to be disrespectful.

See: Feeling Open & Relaxed p.161, Observing Actions & Reactions p.164, Feeling Empathy, Compassion, Gratitude p.167, Practicing Non-Judgment p.169, Softening the Hard Edges p.173

RESPONSIBLE

WHEN YOU TAKE FULL RESPONSIBILITY FOR EVERYTHING YOU
THINK, FEEL, DO, AND SAY, LIFE CEASES TO BE SO CONFUSING

RESPONSIBLE

SELF: For self mastery, the physical, emotional, and mental self all need to be understood and managed. If you responsibly manage the subtleties of mind and character, you can live a life that's free of excessive conflict. Instead of struggling against responsibilities, align them with goals that bring confidence, joy, and meaning.

RELATIONSHIPS: Having a responsible partner means you can depend on someone other than yourself, and help in life is one of the great benefits of a relationship. If responsibilities are ignored, you have to use time and energy to manage conflict rather than meeting intentional goals. People are more free to grow and thrive in relationships where responsible consideration is the norm.

PRACTICE: Watch your thoughts and actions for a week and notice the responsibilities you tend to avoid. Spend time thinking about what needs to be done to make those responsibilities more approachable. For example, you might take one step toward getting something done, so it feels easy to finish the following day, or set a timer and work for small blocks of time so tasks don't seem overwhelming.

See Working with Thoughts or Emotions p.162; Observing Actions & Reactions p.164; Practicing Non-Struggle p.166; Noticing the Space Around Things p.172

REST

THE BEST PRESENT YOU CAN GIVE ANY BUSY ADULT IS
SOME UNINTERRUPTED "ME TIME" BECAUSE IT'S WITHIN
EACH "ME" THAT PEACE AND HAPPINESS IS CULTIVATED.

REST

SELF: There's a time to plan, to act, and to rest. Mindful people address all necessary things in a balanced way, and put attention on one thing at a time. With good rest, the mind is sharp enough to plan and the body is able to act. This seems obvious, but it's easy to complicate simple truths when the mind isn't clear and focused. People who either don't rest, or rest too often are ignoring aspects of their mind-body system.

RELATIONSHIPS: People who know when to act and when to rest are better companions who lead more balanced lives. It's difficult to be around someone who is too stressed out, tired, or wired to be present on an ongoing basis. When you don't balance rest and activity, you may only find comfort in extreme things like addictions or other distractions. Life works better and means more if you balance your time between work, rest, and play.

PRACTICE: Notice if your sleeping and relaxing habits support your energy, or take from it. Does anything need to shift for you to be able to take optimal advantage of downtime? Proactively schedule in work, rest, and play, because your goals and peace of mind depend on balancing everyday life.

See: Beginner's Mind p.160, Coming Back to the Present p.163, Practicing Non-Struggle p.166, Noticing or Deepening the Breath p.168

SHAME

SHAME

SELF: Insecure people use shame to position themselves above others, because they feel powerless themselves. If you shame others, notice how you're probably behaving like a bully you were once shamed by. Shame is not something that defines people, it's a signal that emotions or conflicts need to be worked through in more detail.

RELATIONSHIPS: A 1994 study by Gottman showed signs of contempt to be the highest predictor of divorce within the first 6 years of marriage.[11] To show contempt or to shame a partner is a high level of personal betrayal. There's no practical or justified reason for shaming because it's not constructive, it's just damaging. Shamers are usually "reactors" who haven't reflected enough to understand their own pain and reactions. They impose fear or pain on people without realizing it's because their own shame has been triggered.

PRACTICE: Reflect on moments in your life where you have felt shame. Notice if your energy is stuck in those moments and try to get it moving by breathing in new positive energy as you think of those times. Breathe out old, dark or negative energy that you want to release, and feel your feelings without judgment or shame. You are only human, and nobody gets through life without complications.

See: Working with Thoughts or Emotions p.162, Coming Back to the Present p.163, Practicing Non-Judgment p.169, Feeling Body Sensation & Movements p.170, Opening Heart & Mind p.174

SIMPLICITY

SIMPLICITY

SELF: When things get overly complicated, they take up more time, energy, and head space. You only have so much time, energy and head space to use in a given day. If your life is complicated to the point of tapping out your resources on a regular basis, it's a recipe for chronic stress. Simplicity, on the other hand, has the goal of keeping things uncomplicated, pleasant, and manageable.

RELATIONSHIPS: When people are distracted and stressed, they forget to make room for quality interactions. How you treat people should be given the highest priority, yet this can be ignored when life goes from being simple to complicated. Use practices to simplify the thought traffic in your mind and you'll notice relationships become less confusing because you're more able to focus, understand, and prioritize.

PRACTICE: Think about where you hold clutter in your life. Is it mental, emotional, or physical clutter? Often physical clutter mirrors some cluttered energy within. Or you over-focus on cleanliness to try to balance internal chaos. Work on reducing both external clutter and inner chaos to feel more balanced, inside and out.

See: Beginner's Mind p.160, Working with Thoughts or Emotions p.162, Coming Back to the Present p.163, Dropping Busy Mind p.165, Noticing the Space Around Things p.172

STRUGGLE

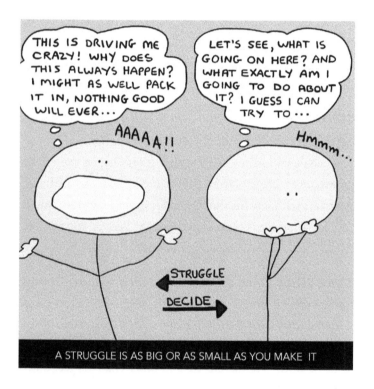

A STRUGGLE IS AS BIG OR AS SMALL AS YOU MAKE IT

STRUGGLE

SELF: You have to believe in a struggle and be willing to engage in it for it to occur. Some people think struggle is a way of life, while others think struggles are rare because problems have solutions (so why struggle)? Detailed awareness of a struggle, beginning with noticing it's there and affecting you, helps you take responsibility for how and why it got there. Struggle is often about not accepting or understanding something. It's also possible to accept "what is," and problem-solve as needed with little or no struggle.

RELATIONSHIPS: Relationships struggle when people fail to address and solve problems before they get over-complicated. Problems build and it becomes increasingly necessary to work around them, in thoughts, feelings, words, and actions. This is much less efficient than accepting problems as real when they occur, and addressing them in the detail necessary to find solutions.

PRACTICE: What would the people in your life say are their greatest struggles? If you are empathetic and compassionate, especially with regard to their greatest struggles, you can improve trust and emotional intimacy in those relationships.

See: Observing Actions & Reactions p.164, Practicing Non-Struggle p.166, Noticing or Deepening the Breath p.168, Practicing Non-Judgment p.169, Softening the Hard Edges p.173

TRUST

IF YOU LOSE TRUST, WHAT WORDS
CAN HELP YOU FIND IT AGAIN?

TRUST

SELF: A mindful outlook requires trust in yourself, others, and life. Without trust, you filter life through a screen of defense that prevents you from giving and receiving in a balanced way. Lack of trust, and the defensive strategies that come with it, may keep out some of the bad, but it keeps out the good as well. If you over-focus on what could go wrong, you're not allowing or enabling things to go right.

RELATIONSHIPS: The quality of love between people depends on the quality of trust between them. Lack of trust prevents the openness required for intimacy to establish, grow, and stay fast in hard times. Trust helps people show their vulnerable side long enough for it to be loved and supported to become strong. When unsure, communicate more to understand who (and how) to trust.

PRACTICE: Practice trusting that your day will unfold exactly as it should. This doesn't mean you'll get everything you want, but that you trust you'll be able to handle whatever comes. If you find this difficult, notice what judgments and fears stand in the way. Should those judgments and fears prevent contentment each day?

See: Beginner's Mind p.160, Feeling Open & Relaxed p.161, Coming Back to the Present p.163, Practicing Non-Struggle p.166, Practicing Non-Judgment p.169, Softening the Hard Edges p.173

VALUES

VALUES

SELF: It's a mindful practice to observe how your everyday life matches up with your values. It's easy to get lost in daily life and focus on things that aren't meaningful, or that don't align with what you believe about yourself. Be mindful of how thoughts, feelings, words, and actions reflect your values, and make adjustments and apologies as needed. If you can be authentic, and give others the respect you like to receive yourself -in each moment- your ethics are probably sound.

RELATIONSHIPS: People who are confused about their values have trouble explaining their behaviour, or they explain it in terms of reacting to others, not in terms of proactive choice. This is a common problem in relationships; blaming the other person, or the circumstance for choices and behaviour. People who've always lived by others' values and choices must learn to define their own, and be more accountable.

PRACTICE: At the end of life, the only thing you have is what kind of person you have been. Define values that will support you to live an honorable life you can enjoy and be proud of.

See: Beginner's Mind p.160, Working with Thoughts or Emotions p.162, Feeling Empathy, Compassion, Gratitude p.167, Noticing the Space Around Things p.172, Opening Heart & Mind p.174

VICTIM

IF THE GREATEST PEOPLE IN HISTORY HAD LET THEIR OPPRESSORS
GET THEM DOWN, WOULD THERE BE ANY GREAT PEOPLE IN HISTORY?

VICTIM

SELF: If people get hurt it's common to feel victimized when apologies or amends aren't forthcoming. If you feel like a victim in your mind, you can try to stop dwelling on the thoughts and feelings about being powerless. You can't always understand the minds and hearts of others, or get a deserved apology, but this only stops you from moving on and living your life if you let it. It's not always easy to move on, but it's a worthy goal to strive for, because your life is for living.

RELATIONSHIPS: In relationships people often feel limited by what others will or won't do. This makes them feel victimized, especially when poor communication makes it hard to solve problems. The way out of the victim's trap is to define the problem and what you intend to do about it yourself. Explain your position and ask others to explain theirs, while you listen. Take space rather than participate in a disrespectful exchange, it's a no-win situation.

PRACTICE: Next time you have a disagreement, continue to be respectful with your words and tone, even if the other person's respect falters. Ask questions, clearly state your position, and create stronger boundaries between yourself and others if necessary. Setting a good example shows strength and confidence, and it may encourage others to behave.

See Working with Thoughts or Emotions p.162; Observing Actions & Reactions p.164; Feeling Empathy, Compassion, Gratitude p.167

VULNERABLE

A HUG IS A HUMAN BANDAGE THAT HOLDS YOUR
VITALS IN PLACE WHEN YOU'RE FEELING VULNERABLE.

VULNERABLE

SELF: Being unwilling to feel or show vulnerability makes you rigid. It shuts down the soft human parts of you. People need to be strong, but also accepting of their own and others' weaknesses. Without vulnerability you're too closed to get to know others, or to let yourself be known by them.

RELATIONSHIPS: People who show both strength and vulnerability feel a wider range of human emotions, and can understand emotions in others as well. A good balance of strength and vulnerability allows for a healthy mix of give and take in relationships.

PRACTICE: When you encounter people who are hard to get along with, think about what vulnerabilities might be under their prickly behaviour. Is it anxiety, insecurity or other fears? When people don't behave well, they're not monsters, they're misguided. Take care of needs and feelings by stating them clearly, and create appropriate boundaries that reflect the degree of trust you have. In close relationships, supporting each other's strengths and vulnerabilities can build intimacy and trust as long as mutual respect remains intact.

See: Feeling Open & Relaxed p.161, Working with Thoughts or Emotions p.162, Feeling Empathy, Compassion, Gratitude p.167, Noticing or Deepening the Breath p.168, Practicing Non-Judgment p.169, Opening Heart & Mind p.174

WANT

WANT

SELF: It's important to balance want with appreciation for what you have. Over-focusing on "what I want next" is a habit that takes the mind away from what's happening now. After each want is attained, attention moves quickly off the formerly cherished want to the next one. If you spend more time chasing things than appreciating them, practice engaging with your moment-by-moment experience more fully on all levels (mental, emotional, physical, spiritual).

RELATIONSHIPS: Many people take those they love for granted. It's easy to over-focus on want or what's missing, and ignore what (and who) you already have. To focus on what's missing from a relationship while not paying enough attention to making things work, is a type of abandonment. If you over-focus on what you want at the expense of current commitments, self-reflect in more detail to understand why, and deal honestly with conflicts between desire, and gratitude for what you have.

PRACTICE: What kinds of things do you want? Are they mental, emotional, physical, or spiritual things? Are they connected to your understanding of what life is about in the grand scheme of things?

See: Working with Thoughts or Emotions p.162, Coming Back to the Present p.163, Observing Actions & Reactions p.164, Feeling Empathy, Compassion, Gratitude p.167

WORRY

WORRY

SELF: Worry isn't an end in itself, and if it's become that, try to mindfully acknowledge and understand your worry habit. Notice a worry in detail without trying to change or solve it. Be curious. Rather than getting caught up in the worry, notice how your mind is working, and how this affects your body, actions, emotions, and focus. Take a break from spinning thoughts by going for a walk outside and feeling your body as it moves, while also focusing on sights or sounds.

RELATIONSHIPS: It is difficult to be around a person who worries, and it's difficult to be a worrier. Worriers jump between fear and control as they grasp for security. Relationship satisfaction depends on being able to relax and trust that problems will be managed as they arise. If worry is a third party in your relationship, it's best to talk openly about how it affects you.

PRACTICE: When a worry is spinning in your mind, focus more on breathing slower and deeper, and feeling your feet on the ground. Write down the worry along with possible action steps to do at particular times. If worries seem unmanageable, seek counselling to improve your quality of life. You don't need to control everything to be okay.

See: Working with Thoughts or Emotions p.162, Noticing or Deepening the Breath p.168, Practicing Non-Judgment p.169, Feeling Body Sensation & Movements p.170

REFLECT, FEEL, AND FOCUS TO PRACTICE MINDFULNESS

Most mindful practices, such as those in this book, are variations on:

1. **Using your senses (and sensations) as a focus** to appreciate life in the moment, and to train yourself out of mental-emotional habits like spinning thoughts, worry, rumination, frustration, anger, helplessness, etc.

2. **Using self-reflection, observation, words or ideas** (mantras), and other active choices to direct your focus, understanding, and behaviour.

In mindful practice, you notice your experience in the moment, without judgment, and interrupt struggle/tension or unconstructive habits if they occur. In time, you form new habits in thoughts/actions/reactions, and eventually in the brain's neural connections as well (ie: new habits are supported by changed physiology in the brain).

Depending on your practice, some possible benefits are: a more peaceful mind, positive self control/confidence on various levels (mental/emotional/physical/spiritual), appreciating more of life as it happens, and being able to direct energy with intention, instead of feeling like past conflicts or current concerns determine everything about who you are, how you feel, and what you do.

'SORT & SOFT' REFLECTIVE AND SENSING PRACTICE

It's often minor struggles such as trying to get out the door on time, feeling tired, or facing a task, that reminds us to switch to mindful mode because mindfulness relieves tension. In time, you will remember to be mindful more often, without having to be triggered by struggle. As you practice, you become familiar with different types of mindful focus, through all kinds of experience. If you're not using mindfulness as an intervention to counter struggle, just begin with the next step (observe) in the practices below.

FOR REFLECTIVE PRACTICES: the word SORT is an acronym to use. You may think about sorting your baggage, or getting your struggles sorted.

(S) Notice a struggle, **(O) observe the moment** and/or the content of your thoughts instead of being caught up in mental or emotional reactions, **(R) reflect on the moment,** your thoughts, emotions, and overall experience, and **(T) train using a mindful practice** to shift toward contentment/peace, and away from unconscious habits, thoughts, or struggles in your mind. Sometimes you'll want to work through a conflict by reflecting, and sometimes you'll just want to gain heightened awareness, reminisce, or enjoy your experience more fully.

FOR SENSING PRACTICES: the word SOFT is an acronym to use. Sensing practices help you shift away from mental **(S)**

struggle (in thoughts), or physical struggles in body tension. **(O) Observe** or put all your attention on **(F) feeling** the breath and body sensations, relaxing tension on purpose and/or **(F) focusing** on something, *without thinking in language.* It works because you shift away from using your left brain (language/worry related) as you **(T) train** your right brain (more sensing than analyzing) to come more online. This helps ground anxious energy, calms the mind, triggers the "relax response" of the nervous system,[12] and feels physically relaxing.

MORE ON...

STRUGGLE . OBSERVE

REFLECT/FEEL/FOCUS

TRAIN

Some longterm goals of the mindful life are to feel content more often, while being effortlessly aware of thoughts, feelings, and actions -moment to moment- as life happens. You can use mindful practice to more fully experience contentment and "flow"[13] when you feel all aspects of yourself are integrated and working together. When this isn't the case, (in moments throughout the day), note you are experiencing tension or struggle, and use a mindful practice to help with it.

STRUGGLE: A struggle occurs. Notice you're struggling. A struggle can be as big as a panic attack, or as small as a vague sense of boredom or an eye twitch. Anything other than relaxation, and perfect inner contentment can be a struggle.

OBSERVE: Shift from being in the middle of your struggle, to observing your struggle. Note how it manifests in your mind and body, and where it may have come from.

REFLECT/FEEL/FOCUS: Reflect on what thoughts led to what emotions and actions to bring on this struggle. With detailed information on what created your struggle, you can problem-solve or choose a suitable practice to interrupt, and calm your struggle or re-direct your focus onto something constructive or pleasing.

Do you need a practice that is more reflective in nature, such as watching thoughts as they occur to understand your frustration, or a practice that is more physical/sensing, such as actively relaxing a body part as you move, or to feel your breath come into your body and leave as you release tension?

Or would you prefer to focus on what you see or hear without labelling it, to bring yourself fully into the moment, and out of your judging, language-based thoughts? When you are proficient at mindful practice, you can do one or more reflective and sensing practices at the same time, if you want to work with both your body and mind at once.

For example, while out for a walk, you might practice the following: feel and relax your shoulders more with each out-breath, and in the background of your attention breathe slower and deeper, while feeling your feet on the ground (to feel sensations of energy come and go from your body as you move). You may also notice thoughts/emotions, or purposely leave your mind open as you simply perceive and feel the moment as it is, without judging or labelling it in words.

TRAIN: Mindful practice is an ongoing training. When you focus your attention in a particular way, "on purpose," your brain builds more capacity to focus that way.[14]

One goal of the mindful life is to feel an effortless contentment more often. You work with thinking habits to make room in your mind for what you want, and also for contentment with "what is." With practice you realize you can make your mind work for you, instead of you for it. Contentment comes with being more aligned with your own mind, body, and vision for this life -moment by moment- instead of having your awareness and behaviour hijacked by habits or internal/external stressors.

FOUR KEY ELEMENTS OF MINDFUL INTELLIGENCE

1. Perspective or emotional maturity shift: Cross the line from being primarily a "reactor" to being an "actor" who takes more proactive responsibility for the mental/emotional/physical self and what it gets up to moment-by-moment. This begins with proactive self-observance, goal-setting, and making more conscious choices about thoughts, feelings and actions.

2. Understand the self within the context of life as a whole, taking your own and others' mortality into account. Knowing you're going to get old and die, what does your life mean? How do you make it meaningful, or explore meaning gradually, while keeping in mind the impermanence of life? When you consciously develop your belief system, it helps you make good choices, instead of living according to cultural, religious, or other expectations you haven't explicitly chosen.

3. Use practices and observations to: appreciate life in the moment; reduce struggle; and adjust thoughts/feelings/behaviour/motives/outcomes to align with values/goals. Practice being more fully present in the moment, while evolving over time. Note that Mindful practice is a *practice*, and it takes many times of shifting away from old mental habits, to make the new ones easier. With practice, you will notice you feel lighter, calm, and joyful more often, as stress is dropped from your mind, energy, and life. You may notice things make sense more easily, and the urge to meditate, pray, or connect to a higher power or purpose that takes you beyond your "self."

There are moments of peace and contentment each time you practice, and one day you will clear your mind with no effort, and know your brain has gotten fully on board to support your mindful habits with shiny new neural connections.

4. Evolve ethically by: reducing negativity, fear and aggression, which tends to limit us, while faith, hope and love tends to open possibilities. There is fear beneath the aggression of every overreaction. Replace fearful (reactive) responses with more respectful loving ones.

Lift the limitations of your negative judgments from your mind to achieve better health, happiness, and positive evolution of all aspects of self (mental/emotional/physical/spiritual). If your guiding principles are to relax, remain optimistic, and respect yourself and others at all times (not as easy as it sounds- every habit and belief will be tested), you will become a Master of Mindful Intelligence.

PART 3

<u>MORE MINDFUL PRACTICES</u>

BEGINNER'S MIND

Beginner's mind[15] is like the openness children have when they encounter new things or face the day with abandon. No goals, expectation, fear, or judgments, just open curiosity. It's being in the moment, open to your senses, to experience life without pre-conceived ideas about how it will unfold.

When you practice Beginner's Mind, the idea is to face all things as if they are new, so you allow space for possibilities instead of letting everything be decided by your expectations or judgments. Approach relationships, conversation, and even mundane activities as if for the first time, and stay open to new feelings and possibilities.

Let one moment lead to the next without expectations while you keep your mind open. Let go of tightly controlling and managing time, the schedule, and others. Be with things as they are in each moment and be patient while allowing life, responses, actions, and sensations to unfold. It's easier to do this if you let go of the idea that everything has to happen instantly or in a rush. It's good to have plans, but it's also important to balance that by letting life come to you.

FEELING OPEN & RELAXED

It's easy to feel tense or closed as you go about your day, and setting an intention to stay open reminds you not to resist things by default. A practice like this shows you where, when, and with whom you are stressed.

You may be unconsciously tensing your shoulders, or not being receptive/relaxed with a particular person. The mind/body and its energy works better with openness, so anywhere you can note tension (rigidity) and relax it out is a step toward better health and wholeness.

Notice if you're hurrying for no reason, or focused on what's next instead of right now. The idea that life has to be lived in a stressful hurry is a product of a culture that's used to perpetual striving. While ambition is valuable, it can also be a problem when it isn't balanced with appreciation for what you already have.

Relax, breathe in, as if through the whole surface of your skin (feel what that feels like), breathe out, as if through the bottom of your feet. Let your feet relax as you feel them in more detail. Repeat. When you relax into your body and the moment, you will notice yourself, and even time, slowing down.

WORKING WITH THOUGHTS OR EMOTIONS

Once you are more aware of yourself and which thoughts (causes) lead to which effects (emotions, actions, reactions), you can make conscious adjustments as needed. Become the detached observer of your train of thought for a period of time, with the goal of noticing thinking habits, or trends in your reactions. You may have songs running through your mind, arguments, conversations, plans, lists, or resentments. You will notice repetitive trends.

Create more space and peace in your mind by not engaging with thoughts that don't improve your quality of life, but take note of anything that points to unresolved conflict so you can investigate further. Spend more time on what you intend, and on just being aware of "what is," in the moment.

Tune into your breath and what you see or hear, or use a phrase to focus away from unwanted thoughts. You may also observe your thoughts from a distance without engaging, and note what needs your attention, then let the rest dissipate as you feel the breath instead.

COMING BACK TO THE PRESENT MOMENT

The mind is always thinking about things, but it's also important to directly experience or feel things. In other words, it's important to get out of your head sometimes. Notice your breath and come back into the present moment where life happens.

To experience more in the present moment, breathe, and notice what's happening through your senses and body sensations as you move. Embodied awareness can make you feel more whole and relaxed (if not, work through emotions that arise). Fully experience the moment, without *thinking about* the moment or needing to judge and label it in words.

Light attention on your breath while you experience the moment helps keep you out of busy thoughts. When you notice you're thinking again (and you will, it's part of the practice), let go of thoughts and come back to the present moment.

Mindful walking[16] and mindful eating[17] are great practices to try because you walk and eat many times a day. Walking and eating can be cues to tune into your breath and body, instead of living in your head in "automatic pilot" mode.

OBSERVING ACTIONS & REACTIONS

Become an observer of your actions and reactions as they happen, for a particular period of time. Notice your assumptions, expectations and motives, in relation to a particular issue or conflict.

As the detached observer, it's easier to see the cause and effect of your actions/reactions. When you become the experiencer, and the observer of your experience at the same time, it can be a relief because you're a step removed from the intensity of the world. The silent watcher within yourself can remain present and calm as circumstances change.

Observe yourself with curiosity and objectivity to see where biases have been clouding your judgment, or preventing you from taking in new information.

Instead of depending on habits, become more flexible and intentional, and you'll notice you feel more free. Life can become more about what you choose moment-to-moment, and you'll have the confidence of knowing what you're doing (and why), more often.

DROPPING BUSY MIND

A busy mind is a constantly active, or ruminating mind. It goes around in circles, or lights on whatever happens along. If your physical body thrashed around the way a busy mind does, you'd be taken to the hospital immediately.[18] The first step toward dropping a busy mind is noticing it's there in the first place.

Observe your train of thought for a period of time, to see how it operates. When you observe the content of random thoughts, it becomes clear you could be putting your mind to better use.

To practice, have an intention to keep a light awareness on your thinking. When you notice you're not consciously choosing thoughts, increase the length of your in-breath and focus your attention completely on one or more of your senses instead (what you hear, what you see, or what you feel). Feel your breath and body sensations as you relax, instead of thinking.

When you interrupt automatic thoughts and re-focus, your brain works on neural connections to make focusing easier. If it's difficult to stop thinking, try to process your emotions,[19] understand behaviour, and adjust coffee, drugs, alcohol, food, sleep, stress, exercise, and time outside.

PRACTICING NON-STRUGGLE

It's easy to be in the habit of resisting things. Some people resist the alarm clock in the morning; worry over breakfast; rant in the car on the way to work; avoid people through the day; scarf down dinner over the sink; drink a bottle of wine and fall into bed, while feeling a perfectly normal day was had.

Others struggle against a never-ending chore list, waiting for the day when they can finally relax. You practice non-struggle to cultivate a feeling of acceptance of yourself, others, and life as it comes, instead of resisting things (mentally, emotionally, physically), for any reason.

Remember (or imagine) what it feels like to be completely open to life, and positive and relaxed as you go about it. Think of it as "cottage mind" or how you feel on holiday when time is your own. Non-struggle is both an idea and a feeling. Relax on purpose, breathe, and stay open instead of being resistant.

Let one moment lead to the next without feeling like you have to judge, over-manage things, or rush. Life is limited and it must be felt and enjoyed now while it lasts, not simply managed or tolerated while you wait for a theoretical better time in the future. Remember, time waits for no one, so be here now!

FEELING EMPATHY, COMPASSION, OR GRATITUDE

Set an intention to practice being empathetic or compassionate toward yourself and the people you meet in a day. You may have one particular person or group you want to focus on, like kids, a parent, spouse, neighbours, pets, co-workers, strangers, or someone you have trouble getting along with.

For another practice, you could approach your day with a feeling of gratitude, trying to remember and appreciate what you have, instead of focusing on what you don't have. A proactive focus or attitude helps you notice, question, and adjust your habitual way of relating. A practice like this often brings new information to light about your habits of thought and behaviour.

Shifting your focus "on purpose" to adjust how you feel, is an important practice for learning to evolve over time. People who practice moving through life with positive thoughts, feelings, and intentions notice there is a physical difference between the 'lightness' of positive feelings and the 'heaviness' of negative feelings. As you become more sensitive to these differences, you naturally lean more toward the positive because it feels better.

NOTICING OR DEEPENING THE BREATH

Noticing the breath is an important practice for any mindful or meditative endeavour. The breath is always with you in the present moment, and focusing on it helps pull your attention out of your train of thought which is often focused on the past or future. Cue yourself[20] to notice and deepen the breath to feel more calm and centered throughout the day. When you're good at focusing on the breath (instead of unconscious thoughts), you can add another focus if you wish.

In mindful practice you often have a light attention on the breath (in the background), while focusing your attention on something else, such as experiencing the moment more fully; relaxing the body; or having intentional thoughts/focus. The breath itself is an interesting focus, reminding you that nothing in life is permanent due to its nature of coming and going.

Think about bringing things into your life on the in-breath, and letting things go on the out-breath. Whereas stress causes shallow breathing, slow deep breathing calms you down, slows your heart rate, and trips your nervous system into the relax response[21] more often.

PRACTICING NON-JUDGMENT

The categorizing human brain likes to put people and things into categories so it will know what to expect. This is one reason why it's common to criticize and judge even when there's no good reason for doing it. Unnecessary judgment takes up a lot of space in your mind that could be better used for experiencing peace and quiet, or doing something constructive.

You can practice non-judgment by setting an intention for the day or week to stop judging/labelling. This doesn't mean you can't form opinions, it means when you notice yourself labelling things as good/bad, fat/thin, ugly/pretty, i hate it/i love it, etc, you question whether it's necessary, then drop it from your train of thought when it's not.

It is also easy to judge and criticize others because it helps you avoid thinking about yourself and your own problems. There's plenty to clean up in your own mind and life, so if you notice your focus is on managing or criticizing others, look within for the fears driving your self-avoidance. Non-judgment can help you achieve more balance by quieting the left brain, which governs language. Bring the right brain more online by sensing things in your body and environment. Breathe, feel, and notice more, judge less.

FEELING BODY SENSATION, MOVEMENT & BALANCE

Tune into the breath (and out of your thoughts) and feel your body as you sit, stand, or move through the day. Notice if you feel heaviness, tension or pain.

Breathe and focus attention into a tense spot on your in-breath, and relax it fully on your out-breath. Notice tingling sensations or shooting pains as you relax out tension. Don't resist them, as this is your body opening up tension and letting things (blood, lymph, energy or qi) flow again.

Keep a light attention on your breath in the background as you relax and notice your posture while you walk, sit, or stand. Breathe energy/light into your body (feel it, don't think about it), and relax more on each out-breath as you settle your body into feeling more balanced.

Feeling your breath and body at the same time grounds your energy. When grounded, your energy flows better (in and out), and stays topped up as you move through the day. Practice this to prevent you from carrying stress, or feeling "drained" at the end of the day. Take life one breath, one sensation at a time.

NOTICING SOUND, COLOUR, OR SHAPES

Take a walk, tune into your breath (and out of your thoughts), and focus on one of these without thinking: Let sounds come to your ears; let what you see come to your eyes (passively, as if you're watching a movie); notice just colour; or notice just shapes. Keep a light attention on slower deeper breathing in the background. Note how you feel before and after each practice.

This practice shows you it's possible to control what to focus on. New neural pathways are forged in the brain when you focus attention in different ways, so sense and feel as you breathe and practice, without thinking, to give language-based neurons a break. Even a few moments makes a difference to how you feel.

Shift away from words or thoughts built from language, onto sights, sounds, or sensations, to relieve an over-busy, ruminating mind. On the other hand, if you're more emotional than logical, it can help to use words to identify feelings, or to create a mantra that counters distractions, such as "be here now" or "breathe and feel." Each time you interrupt and calm "scattered mind" and then shift focus, you train your brain to perceive more, to be intentional, and improve your quality of life.

NOTICING THE SPACE AROUND THINGS

The world is made up of things that are both "there" and "not there." It can be relieving to the mind to stop actively focusing for a while, and to notice the space around things. It can encourage a change of perspective to focus more on emptiness, especially if you have spinning thoughts or a stressful busy life. It's easier for busy thoughts to clear while focusing on the breath and a loose awareness of the space around things.

The mind and body can become cluttered with tensions throughout the day, and these can be noticed, felt, and then released, while tuning into the space around things. Breathe in emptiness or light energy, then relax and breathe out clutter, darkness, or heaviness from your mind and body. You may even notice a physically relieving sensation in your head while doing this practice.

This is a good practice to do after work, while walking outside, or before bed to release the tensions of the day. Philosophically speaking, noticing the space around things can remind you to stop obsessing about material things, and pay attention to life's intangibles such as meaning, spirit, peace, and love.

SOFTENING THE HARD EDGES

The "hard edges" are physical tensions, judgments, fears or anything that feels hard and closed rather than soft and open. Cultivate a feeling of softness inside your body and mind by relaxing completely. Use a visualization if it helps, then try to feel the softness in your body, as you breathe. For example, your entire body and mind is filled with a gentle breeze, warm liquid, or the sound and feel of waves on a warm beach. Breathe in softness and light, and breathe out tensions as you relax.

Try to feel the softness in your whole body out to the surface of your skin for several breaths. Then let the softness extend out past your skin as you continue to follow your breath, and feel what it's like to be bigger than the confines of your body. The softer you feel on the inside, the longer it will take for tensions to accumulate and bring you to a reaction or feeling of intense irritation.

You can tell a lot about people by the way they move or hold their bodies. Notice tensions you are holding, whether they are mental, emotional, or physical, and try to soften them up. Notice how tension or softness affects your posture, words, and body language, and try to feel more soft and open on the inside.

OPEN HEART & MIND

Set an intention to give and receive more love, and remain open to new ideas. A practice like this helps show you where your biases are. It may also show where you're closing down unnecessarily or using old defenses that are no longer relevant or needed.

Maybe you're not allowing yourself to give or receive love and support. There's a feeling of lightness that comes with opening the heart and mind which you can try to feel in your chest and head during this practice. Tune into the breath and imagine you're clearing the heaviness in your head and chest with each breath in. On the out-breath relax and release tension. Another variation is to feel like you're breathing into your chest/head and breathe out, as if through the soles of your feet.

Practically speaking this feels like your head and chest open up, and your feet feel more heavy and relaxed on the ground as energy releases (they may tense up first before they relax, just allow it to happen without resisting).

Give and receive little connections like a nod or a smile as you meet people through the day. Try to cultivate a feeling of curiosity and freedom, to counter habitual responses, and feel the joy that comes from having an open, receptive approach to life.

ENDNOTES

1. It's often considered necessary to take a non-judgmental inventory of flaws, as a necessary step for growth or healing.

Aaron B. Murray-Swank , Kelly M. McConnell & Kenneth I. Pargament (2007) Understanding spiritual confession: A review and theoretical synthesis, Mental Health, Religion & Culture, 10:3, 275-291, DOI: 10.1080/13694670600665628

Hymer, Sharon. Springer, 1995, Therapeutic and Redemptive Aspects of Religious Confession, pp 41-54

Brown, Brené. (2022). The Gifts of Imperfection.

2. Writing in this book is addressed more toward Western cultures. Mindfulness applies to people of all cultures, but in different ways, depending on beliefs, attitudes, and other frames of reference.

3. **Berkeley News, Despite drift toward authoritarianism, Trump voters stay loyal. Why? Edward Lempinen, Dec, 2020**

https://news.berkeley.edu/2020/12/07/despite-drift-toward-authoritarianism-trump-voters-stay-loyal-why

Summary, Trump 2023-2024: As of Spring 2024, in the run-up to the 2024 US election, in addition to regularly using hate speech and bullying/threats against political and business opponents, Donald Trump (45th President of the United

States Jan 2017-2020) admitted to sexual assaults on a network television video out-take which was used in a court case to help convict him of sexual assault, he publicly and politically aligned himself with Dictators such as Vladimir Putin and Kim Jong Un, and was involved in numerous legal battles involving issues ranging from sex crimes and various forms of financial fraud to inciting violence/insurrection, vote tampering (in an attempt to overturn 2020 election results), and mishandling classified documents.

These facts were well known to those who supported him to continue as leader of the Republican Party in the USA and try for a second term as President in 2024.

4. These connected thoughts/feelings/actions can become automatic reactions if you aren't choosing thoughts and behaviours "on purpose."

From Goran Simic et al, "Understanding Emotions: Origins and Roles of the Amygdala" Biomolecules, Jun, 2021. published online 2021 May 31. doi: 10.3390/biom11060823

Excerpt: Emotions can be understood only in the context of adaptive, synchronized interactions of widely distributed cortical and subcortical neural networks that mediate complex adaptive behaviours, such as perception, cognition, motivation, and actions in which the amygdala plays a central modulatory role. Human intelligence arises from the complex interaction of cognitive processes that are modified by different levels of emotional self-awareness and motivation. Awareness of one's emotions and feelings and the ability to empathize and use judgment are required abilities and skills to enable cognitive embodiment, social awareness and self-regulation of cognitive processes.

5. neuroplasticity

Rugnetta,   Michael.   "neuroplasticity". Encyclopedia   Britannica,   1   Nov.   2023, https://www.britannica.com/science/neuroplasticity. Accessed 9 November 2023.

Excerpt: Neuroplasticity, capacity of neurons and neural networks in the brain to change their connections and behaviour in response to new information, sensory stimulation, development, damage, or dysfunction. Although some neural functions appear to be hard-wired in specific, localized regions of the brain, certain neural networks exhibit modularity and carry out specific functions while also retaining the capacity to deviate from their usual functions and to reorganize themselves. Hence, neuroplasticity is considered generally to be a complex, multifaceted, fundamental property of the brain.

Also from:

Harvard Health Publishing, Can Mindfulness Change Your Brain, Andrew E. Budson, MD, Harvard Medical School, May 13, 2021

https://www.health.harvard.edu/blog/can-mindfulness-change-your-brain-202105132455

Excerpt: ... (by) focusing on the present moment, cultivating mindful awareness toward sensations, and attending to the rising and falling of the breath, you can actually improve your brain's ability to direct your attention and accurately perceive the world.

It used to be thought that components of thinking that make up your IQ, such as attention, were relatively fixed because they are based upon your brain's function. However, from studies like this one, we now understand that is an old-fashioned idea. By practicing cognitive skills such as mindfulness, you can literally change your mind, your brain, and your IQ.

6. Daniel Goleman, Richard Davidson, Altered Traits; What the Science Reveals about how Meditation Changes Your Mind, Brain, and Body (New York: Penguin Random House, 2017) p 251

Daniel Goleman is author of Emotional Intelligence: Why It Can Matter More Than IQ, the Groundbreaking Bestseller, and many other books on Emotional Intelligence and why it matters. See his info about a brain study on "olympic level meditators."

https://bigthink.com/the-well/high-level-meditators/

7. Jill Bolte Taylor might describe it as spending more time in your right brain.

Jill Bolte Taylor is a Neuroscientist (Neuroanatomist) who suffered a traumatic brain bleed which shut down much of her left brain functioning for some time, resulting in her feeling as if she was "in bliss," experiencing her "self" as having no boundaries, either physical, or the typical constraints of the judgmental, rational mind (ie: she was spending all her time in the right brain). She survived, and regained much of her functioning through rehabilitation, and wrote the books "My Stroke of Insight" and "Whole Brain Living." She was also the author/speaker of the first "Ted Talk" (https://en.wikipedia.org/wiki/TED_(conference) to go viral on the internet.

8. Thich Nhat Hanh

Thich Nhat Hanh was a Buddhist Monk, activist, author, and prolific writer on the subject of Mindfulness. He was well known for teaching (and living) engaged Buddhism, and Mindfulness in everyday life. He was nominated by Martin Luther King Jr. for the Nobel Peace Prize after his many peacekeeping ventures and supportive measures (and refusing to take sides) during the Vietnam war. He was a beloved teacher and when he practiced Mindful Walking, it looked as if he was gliding effortlessly over the earth because every movement was both relaxed and intentional.

9. Competitive thinking

From: Goodtherapy, Communication: Competitive vs Cooperative, Jim Hutt PhD, May 27 2011 https://www.goodtherapy.org/blog/communication-competit ive-versus-cooperative/

Competitive Communication:

• Adversarial: you vs me

• Winners and losers

- Objective is to win vs being happy

- Objective is to be right vs being happy

- No resolution

- Builds distance between partners

- No room for negotiation

- Fundamentally rigid/inflexible

Cooperative Communication:

- You each work together for common goals

- No individual winners or losers- both "win"

- Objective is to understand each others' experience and find common ground

- Objective is to learn about the other and ones self

- Resolution is paramount

- Builds intimacy and closeness

- Fundamentally flexible and open

10. access to energy others don't have access to.

Advanced spiritual practitioners or saints of all major religions have been said/documented to have attained skills that are considered supernatural to the average person, such as omniscient awareness, incorruptibility, ability to heal, levitation, and prophecy. As an advanced meditator you may begin to notice more clarity for solving problems, that solutions present themselves in seeming coincidence, and the ongoing sense of being connected to an energy greater than your own body. These signs along with a sense of peace and well-being propel people forward in meditation practice and the quest for enlightenment/wisdom.

—See the text Autobiography of a Yogi by Paramahansa Yogananda for accounts involving people affected by energy at a distance, appearance/disappearance of objects, being in two places at once, knowledge of time of death, darshan (being positively affected by the energy of a holy person by being near them) incorruptibility, prophetic dreams and messages, healing ability, ability to live without food or drink, and more.

11. Gottman re: contempt and divorce:

Gottman JM. What predicts divorce: The relationship between marital processes and marital outcomes. Hillsdale, NJ: Erlbaum; 1994.

12. relax response of the nervous system

From: Harvard Health Publishing, Understanding the Stress Response July 6, 2020, Harvard Medical School. https://www.health.harvard.edu/staying-healthy/understandi ng-the-stress-response

Relaxation response. Dr. Herbert Benson, director emeritus of the Benson-Henry Institute for Mind Body Medicine at

Massachusetts General Hospital, has devoted much of his career to learning how people can counter the stress response by using a combination of approaches that elicit the relaxation response. These include deep abdominal breathing, focus on a soothing word (such as peace or calm), visualization of tranquil scenes, repetitive prayer, yoga, and tai chi.

Most of the research using objective measures to evaluate how effective the relaxation response is at countering chronic stress have been conducted in people with hypertension and other forms of heart disease. During that second phase, 50% were able to eliminate at least one blood pressure medication — significantly more than in the control group, where only 19% eliminated their medication.

Vingerhoets AJ. The role of the parasympathetic division of the autonomic nervous system in stress and the emotions. Int J Psychosom. 1985;32(3):28-34. PMID: 3902696.

Benson, H., Beary, J. F., & Carol, M. P. (1974). The relaxation response. Psychiatry: Journal for the Study of Interpersonal Processes, 37(1), 37–46.

13. Flow

Csikszentmihalyi, Mihaly. Flow: The Psychology of Optimal Experience. New York, Harper & Row, 1990.

Psychologist Mihaly Csikszentmihalyi's famous investigations of "optimal experience" have revealed that what makes an experience genuinely satisfying is a state of consciousness called flow. During flow, people typically experience deep enjoyment, creativity, and a total involvement with life. In this new edition of his groundbreaking classic work, Csikszentmihalyi demonstrates the ways this positive state can be controlled, not just left to chance. Flow: The Psychology of Optimal Experience teaches how, by ordering the information that enters our consciousness, we can discover true happiness and greatly improve the quality of our lives.

14. When you focus your attention in a particular way, "on purpose," your brain builds more capacity to focus.

See notes 4,5,6,12,13

15. Beginner's Mind

The concept in Zen Buddhism (shoshin), means "beginner's mind." Shoshin refers to the idea of letting go of your preconceptions and having an attitude of openness.

Suzuki, Shunryū and Trudy Dixon. Zen Mind, Beginner's Mind. 1st ed., 16th printing. New York, Weatherhill, 1982.

16. Mindful Walking

Mindful walking is an important type of mindful practice that involves focusing your attention on the senses, body sensations, a particular mental focus and/or movements while walking. Mindful walking helps you go into mindful practice/focus throughout the day, while on the move.

17. Mindful Eating

Mindful eating is a practice of being fully aware of your food and senses while eating, to experience eating more fully instead of being on "autopilot."

18. If your physical body thrashed about the way a busy mind does, you'd be taken to the hospital immediately.

I once attended a talk on mindfulness in Kitchener Ontario, Canada, by a Buddhist Nun, whose name I don't recall, but she said something to this effect, and it always stuck with me, so I'd like to credit her with the statement. I don't know if she read it somewhere or came up with it on her own, but it's very insightful, about what seems permissible in the mind due to the fact that it is private.

19. Process emotions:

Think about an emotional pain or vulnerability, or a memory that bothers you. Allow yourself to experience your feelings without censoring yourself, and without tensing up or resisting (in your mind or body), then release the heavy/stuck energy as you release emotion. Try breathing slower and deeper as you think about a memory or feel an emotional pain from the past, and "relax into" the pain or emotion that arises instead of tensing physically or resisting it in any way. When you think about giving or receiving proper kindness, care, help and attention to your emotional pain (and feeling what that would feel like), it can help bring stuck emotions to the surface so they can be released.

See abstract on embodied memories: Ianì, F. (2019). Embodied memories: Reviewing the role of the body in memory processes. Psychonomic Bulletin & Review, 26(6), 1747–1766. https://doi.org/10.3758/s13423-019-0167

https://www.cambridge.org/core/books/abs/embodied-groun ding/embodiment-of-emotion/8FD8A1FDCB8ACC6C0CF 84FB464722DD5 Embodied Grounding Social, Cognitive, Affective, and Neuroscientific Approaches , pp. 237 - 262 DOI: https://doi.org/10.1017/CBO9780511805837.011 Publisher: Cambridge University Press Print publication year: 2008

20. Cue yourself

Choose cues in your everyday life which will be hard to miss, that remind you to notice your breathing. It's common to breathe very shallow or to hold your breath when stressed, or to breathe in an irregular pattern.

Cue yourself to slow and deepen your breath at points throughout the day. Some examples of cues are every time you: open a door; open the fridge; walk to the bathroom; get up from your desk; shut the car door or click your seat belt; feel annoyed/stressed; hear the kids; pick up your phone; set down your phone; eat; or do menial tasks.

You may also place stickers or other visual cues around your home or work that will catch your eye, reminding you to tune into the breath. You can set a reminder on your phone at regular intervals until you're able to cue yourself.

In time, deeper slower breathing and feeling the body instead of thinking becomes a positive, proactive habit that doesn't require external cues. When you feel your feet on the ground, sit at your desk, or feel body movements as you walk, you will eventually be automatically cued to tune into your breath. This practice helps you remain present and relaxed throughout the day, instead of allowing stress to build, or unconscious habits to take over.

21. Relax response

See note 12

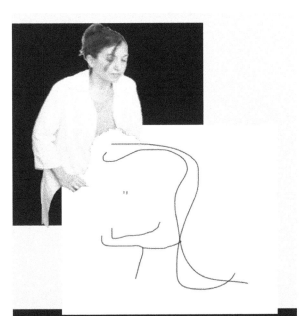

Tracy Rowan has been a Counsellor since 2006, and is also an Acupuncturist. Teaching mindfulness is an integral part of her practice because the reality of the self, and what's important in life, becomes clear with mindful attention (and descriptive cartoons).

Go to MindfulontheMove.com. Follow our app to go more in depth into mindfulness practice. Learn to be mindful on the move, and make the world a better place by inviting friends to do the same! Practice mindfulness one breath, one choice at a time, and find out first hand how Mindful Intelligence can be the making of you.